Risk
Management Essentials
A Handbook for Financial Stability

By
Nathan Venture, D

Risk
Management Essentials
A Handbook for Financial Stability

Table of Contents

Introduction

Investment isn't for the faint of heart. Whether you're an individual investor, a financial planner, or a corporate finance professional, understanding and managing investment risks is essential. The financial landscape is a labyrinth of opportunities and pitfalls, and this book aims to guide you through it with a mix of expository insight, practical advice, and motivational flair. Our goal is to equip you with the knowledge and strategies to safeguard your investments, diversify your portfolio, and enhance your risk tolerance.

Why focus on risk? Because risk is the bedrock upon which all investment decisions are made. It's the variable that can turn a promising venture into a cautionary tale or transform a steady portfolio into a stress-free retirement fund. For experienced investors and newcomers alike, grasping the fundamentals of risk management is crucial for making informed, confident decisions.

Our exploration starts with a fundamental question: What exactly is investment risk? Understanding the nature of risk—its forms, sources, and impacts—is the first step toward managing it effectively. We'll delve into the principles of risk management, uncovering how to identify and assess various risks, and explore strategies to respond to them appropriately. These foundational elements set the stage for everything that follows.

But knowledge alone isn't enough. This book will also show you how to translate risk assessment into practical, actionable strategies. You'll learn to evaluate your risk tolerance and create personalized investor profiles, allowing for customized risk management approaches that suit your unique needs and goals. We'll also discuss the significant role of asset diversification—both in theory and practice. Diversification isn't just a buzzword; it's a proven method for spreading risk and enhancing returns.

In today's data-driven world, quantitative analysis plays a pivotal role in risk management. Statistical tools, modeling techniques, and scenario analyses provide valuable insights, transforming raw data into actionable intelligence. However, numbers alone don't tell the whole story. Qualitative considerations, such as behavioral biases and risk perception, are equally crucial.

Market risk and volatility are ever-present concerns in the financial sector. Understanding how to measure and manage these risks through hedging strategies and other instruments is vital for stability and growth. Similarly, credit risk and counterparty exposure are integral to the broader risk management picture. Effective identification and mitigation strategies can protect against unforeseen financial fallout.

Operational risk often gets overlooked, but it's just as critical. Assessing operational risk, implementing control mechanisms, and planning for recovery are key components of a robust risk management strategy. Legal and regulatory compliance is another area where vigilance is necessary. Navigating the complex web of financial regulations requires a solid understanding of how compliance intersects with risk management.

There's also room for advanced techniques in your risk management toolkit. Dynamic hedging, derivatives, stress testing, and extreme value theory offer sophisticated methods for navigating an unpredictable market. By analyzing real-world case studies, you'll see how these theories and strategies play out in practice, illustrating both successes and cautionary tales.

The integration of risk management into business operations is where theory meets practice. This holistic approach ensures that risk considerations permeate every level of decision-making, from the boardroom to the trading floor. As you progress through this book, you'll gain a comprehensive understanding that prepares you to tackle the complexities of modern finance.

In closing, this book is designed to be a beacon of knowledge and a practical guide. It combines the rigor of quantitative analysis with the nuance of qualitative insights, creating a comprehensive resource for anyone involved in investment and financial decision-making. By the time you reach the conclusion, you'll not only be well-versed in risk management principles but also inspired to apply them effectively. Welcome to a journey that promises to transform your approach to investments, enhance your risk tolerance, and ultimately, safeguard your financial future.

Chapter 1:
Understanding Risk Management

The cornerstone of any successful investment strategy is a deep understanding of risk management. Risk, by its very nature, is an inherent part of investing and cannot be entirely avoided; rather, it can be identified, assessed, and strategically mitigated. This chapter sets the stage for navigating the complex landscape of risk by delving into its fundamental concepts. We begin by defining what investment risks are, highlighting their multifaceted nature that ranges from market volatility to credit and operational risks. The role of risk in financial decision-making is pivotal—whether you're an investor, financial planner, or economic analyst, knowing how to manage and leverage risk effectively can transform potential pitfalls into opportunities for growth. This understanding equips you with the foresight to make informed decisions, balance your portfolio, and ultimately, achieve your financial goals. Let's embark on this journey to unravel the intricacies of risk and arm ourselves with the knowledge to manage it wisely.

Defining Investment Risks

This entails understanding the myriad ways in which investments can potentially lose value, underscoring the importance of strategic planning and informed decision-making. Each type of risk presents unique challenges that investors must navigate to protect and grow their portfolios effectively.

Firstly, market risk, also known as systematic risk, arises from the inherent fluctuations in the financial markets. These are the types of risks that can't be eliminated through diversification. Market risks are influenced by macroeconomic factors such as interest rate changes, political instability, economic recessions, and global events. The 2008 financial crisis is a quintessential example, where market-wide panic led to plummeting asset values globally. For investors, understanding market risk means recognizing that no matter how diversified your portfolio may be, broader economic factors will still exert influence.

Credit risk is another significant type of investment risk. This occurs when borrowers, whether they be corporations or governments, fail to meet their debt obligations. For instance, if you've invested in corporate bonds, there's always the chance that the company may default on its payments. Historical cases like the Enron scandal highlight how devastating credit risk can be. Credit ratings and credit default swaps are tools used to gauge and mitigate this risk, ensuring that investors are aware of the likeliness of default by the issuers.

Next, we have liquidity risk, which pertains to the investor's ability to quickly buy or sell an asset without causing a significant impact on its price. This can be particularly problematic in times of market stress when finding a buyer for your assets can be challenging. Imagine holding investments in real estate or certain small-cap stocks; these assets may not be easily sold without accepting a lower price, especially in volatile markets. Liquidity risk necessitates a good understanding of market conditions and the underlying assets to avoid scenarios where you're stuck with unsellable investments.

Operational risk originates from an organization's internal failures, including inadequate systems, human errors, and mismanagement. For investors, operational risks can affect stock prices and company performance significantly. For example, a cybersecurity breach can lead not only to financial losses but also to a loss of consumer confidence, thereby impacting the organization's valuation. Investors need to monitor a company's operational soundness to prevent potential negative impacts on their investment.

Moreover, we mustn't overlook regulatory risk. This risk arises when changes in laws and regulations can impact the profitability or even the viability of an investment. For example, stricter environmental regulations can increase production costs for manufacturing companies. By keeping abreast of policy changes and lobbying efforts, investors can better anticipate and respond to these risks.

Interest rate risk is crucial mainly for fixed-income investments like bonds. When interest rates rise, existing bonds with lower rates become less attractive, leading to a drop in their market value. Conversely, falling interest rates can result in higher prices for existing bonds. Understanding the cyclical nature of interest rates can aid investors in timing their bond investments more effectively.

Then, there is inflation risk, the danger that inflation will erode purchasing power over time, decreasing the real value of investment returns. Assets like stocks and real estate often provide a hedge against inflation, while fixed-income investments may suffer. The early 1980s saw rampant inflation in the U.S., affecting everything from consumer goods to investment portfolios. It's crucial for investors to include inflation considerations into their risk assessment processes.

Another aspect to consider is geopolitical risk, which emerges from political instability, conflicts, and international relations. These can have far-reaching effects on global markets, commodity prices, and investment environments. An example is the impact of Brexit on the financial markets, causing significant volatility and changing the investment landscape for numerous sectors. Geopolitical risk requires continual monitoring of global news and an awareness of international developments that can affect investments.

Reputational risk, often overlooked, can be just as critical. For instance, if a company is involved in a scandal, it can suffer a severe drop in stock price as consumer trust and brand loyalty wane. Investing in companies with strong governance and ethical standards can help mitigate this type of risk.

Finally, we should consider specific risks endemic to particular investment types. Real estate investing, for example, involves unique risks like property devaluation, changes in local housing markets, and tenant defaults. Commodity investments are subject to risks such as supply chain disruptions and price volatility due to factors like weather patterns and political instability in producing regions.

Understanding these diverse investment risks is crucial for developing robust risk management strategies. It's about balancing potential rewards with corresponding risks, staying informed, and adapting to market changes. By grasping these concepts, investors, financial planners, and asset managers can make more informed decisions, aligning their strategies with their financial goals and risk tolerance.

Defining Investment Risks isn't just about identifying each risk separately but appreciating their interconnectedness and cumulative impact on portfolios. The goal is to equip you with a holistic understanding to navigate the unpredictable terrain of investing more confidently and successfully.

The Role of Risk in Financial Decision Making

This cannot be underestimated. Risk is, after all, the heartbeat of finance, influencing every decision, from portfolio construction to daily trading strategies. For investors and finance professionals, understanding risk is paramount. It acts as a compass guiding decisions in an environment that's inherently uncertain and unpredictable. To navigate this maze successfully, one must appreciate the different types of risk and their implications on financial outcomes.

At its core, risk represents the possibility that actual returns on an investment will deviate from expected returns. This deviation can be both positive and negative, but in financial parlance, risk is often associated with the downside—the potential for loss. It's crucial to recognize just how integral risk is to the financial decision-making process, essentially because no reward comes without it. The art of investing is not about avoiding risk but about managing it effectively to achieve desired financial goals.

Integrating risk into financial decisions requires a robust framework for evaluation and mitigation. This begins with a thorough understanding of different types of risks, such as market risk, credit risk, operational risk, and liquidity risk, each demanding unique strategies for assessment and control. For instance, market risk, the risk of losses due to movements in market prices, can be mitigated through diversification and hedging strategies, whereas credit risk, the risk of a counterparty's default, might necessitate stringent credit assessments and risk-adjusted lending rates.

Moreover, risk is not a static concept. It evolves with changing market dynamics, economic conditions, and advancements in financial theories and instruments. Financial professionals must stay agile, continuously updating their risk management strategies to align with the latest developments. The 2008 financial crisis, for example, underscored the catastrophic consequences of underestimating systemic risk and taught valuable lessons in the importance of comprehensive risk assessment.

Risk also plays a pivotal role in shaping an individual's investment strategy. For instance, a risk-averse investor may favor bonds and other fixed-income securities that offer lower returns but higher security. Meanwhile, a risk-tolerant investor might lean towards equities or alternative investments such as cryptocurrencies, which come with higher volatility but also the potential for greater gains. Understanding one's risk tolerance is, therefore, a fundamental aspect of financial planning and decision-making.

Beyond individual portfolios, risk assessment impacts corporate finance decisions, such as capital structure optimization and project valuation. Companies constantly evaluate financial risk to determine the optimal mix of debt and equity financing, aiming to minimize their cost of capital while maximizing shareholder wealth. In project valuation, risk assessment tools like Discounted Cash Flow (DCF) analysis incorporate risk-adjusted discount rates to ensure that projected cash flows adequately reflect the underlying uncertainties.

Economic analysts and policy makers also weave risk considerations into broader macroeconomic policies. They monitor systemic risk—risks that can trigger widespread instability in the financial system—and take preemptive measures to prevent financial contagion. Tools like stress testing and scenario analysis enable them to simulate adverse economic conditions and evaluate the resilience of financial institutions.

For asset managers and portfolio managers, the ability to quantify risk using sophisticated financial models and statistical tools is invaluable. They employ Value at Risk (VaR) models, Monte Carlo simulations, and other stochastic methods to predict the potential for loss and adjust their portfolios accordingly. These quantitative techniques, combined with qualitative insights, enable a balanced approach to risk management.

Additionally, risk is embedded in the regulatory environment. Legal and regulatory compliance forms a backbone for sustainable financial practices. Financial regulations set the ground rules for risk management, compelling institutions to adhere to stringent capital adequacy ratios, maintain transparent reporting practices, and conduct rigorous internal audits. Non-compliance can result in severe penalties, tarnish reputations, and even lead to financial insolvency.

Traders, facing the daily ebb and flow of market movements, are perhaps the most immediate beneficiaries of an in-depth understanding of risk. They develop strategies that range from simple stop-loss orders to complex algorithmic trading models to mitigate daily risks. The ability to react rapidly to market signals and manage risks in real-time enhances their ability to profit sustainably.

Financial educators and students can't overlook the significance of risk in financial curricula. Theories of risk and return, portfolio theory, capital asset pricing models, and derivatives are staples in finance education, providing the foundational knowledge future professionals need to innovatively tackle the complexities of financial risk.

Risk management isn't just about protection; it's about opportunity. Effective risk management enables businesses and investors to seize opportunities that might otherwise be seen as too perilous. It transforms uncertainties into strategic decisions, each calculated and measured for maximum potential and minimal downside.

Understanding the intricate roles that different types of risks play can embolden investors and financial professionals to make informed, confident decisions. By integrating comprehensive risk management practices, they are not merely safeguarding their assets—they are paving the way for sustained growth and financial health. Every financial model, strategy, and tool developed is a testament to the central role risk plays in shaping sound financial decisions.

Ultimately, appreciating and managing risk is what sets apart the successful investor from the rest. It's about striking that perfect balance between caution and audacity, knowing when to act and when to hold back. In the ever-evolving landscape of finance, a nuanced understanding of risk is not just a skill—it's a necessity.

Chapter 2:
Principles of Risk Management

Effective risk management is a cornerstone of financial success, anchored in identifying, assessing, and mitigating potential threats to investment portfolios. Fundamental principles guide practitioners in navigating these complexities, integrating an understanding of potential risks with strategic responses that align with overall financial goals. By employing a systematic approach, investors and financial professionals can anticipate uncertainties and develop robust strategies to protect and grow their assets. These principles not only emphasize the importance of vigilance and proactive planning but also highlight the necessity of flexibility and adaptation in the face of evolving market dynamics. Ultimately, mastering these principles empowers you to sustain performance and seize opportunities, ensuring your financial endeavors are resilient against the vicissitudes of the market.

Risk Identification and Assessment

This is the foundation of effective risk management. It serves as your initial diagnostic tool, enabling you to pinpoint potential threats and vulnerabilities early in the investment process. This proactive measure is crucial; without identifying and understanding risks, it's challenging to develop strategies to mitigate them. Hence, this phase should never be underestimated.

Beginning with risk identification, investors and financial professionals should thoroughly scour the landscape for various forms of risk. These risks can be categorized broadly into market risk, credit risk, operational risk, and legal/regulatory risks, among others. Through a detailed identification process, you not only unveil obvious risks but also uncover those that might be lurking under the surface. This comprehensiveness is vital, as unidentified risks can derail even the best-laid investment plans.

A valuable method for risk identification is brainstorming sessions with your team. Gather diverse perspectives—analysts, portfolio managers, financial planners—to discuss potential risks. Diversity in thought processes helps to produce a more exhaustive list of dangers that your investments might encounter. Additionally, leveraging technologies such as risk management software and data analytics can provide substantial assistance in spotlighting hidden risks.

Once risks are identified, the next logical step is to assess them meticulously. This assessment involves analyzing the likelihood of each risk and the magnitude of its potential impact on your portfolio. Probability evaluation employs both quantitative methods, such as statistical models, and qualitative judgments based on experience and market insights. It's an intricate balance—overestimating risks can lead to excessive hedging, while underestimating them leaves you exposed.

Each risk's potential impact must be gauged thoroughly. This can be achieved using scenario analysis, where various hypothetical situations are simulated to understand the ramifications of each risk if it materializes. Scenario analysis can reveal insights about how different risks interact and compound each other, providing a holistic view of the threat landscape. For high-risk scenarios, conducting stress tests ensures that even extreme situations are considered.

It's crucial to remember that risk assessment isn't a one-time activity. Instead, it's a continual process requiring regular monitoring and updates. Market conditions evolve, emerging risks appear, and existing risks morph with time. Therefore, a systematic approach to reassessing risks at predetermined intervals is indispensable for maintaining a resilient risk management framework.

In parallel with these identification and assessment activities, maintaining a risk register is a best practice. This document systematically records all identified risks, the assessments made, and the mitigation steps proposed. It serves as a living document, accessible to all team members, ensuring transparency and collective accountability.

One effective tool within the assessment arsenal is risk rating. By assigning a numerical score based on probability and impact, risks can be classified into categories such as high, medium, or low. This ranking clarifies which risks demand immediate attention and which can be monitored over the longer term. Visual aids like risk matrices can provide additional clarity, helping stakeholders to quickly grasp the overall risk landscape.

Advanced techniques like value at risk (VaR) and conditional value at risk (CVaR) can also be employed for more precise assessment. VaR estimates the maximum potential loss over a specified period at a given confidence level, while CVaR provides an assessment of tail risks beyond the VaR threshold. These techniques, while sophisticated, offer valuable insights and aid in making informed decisions on capital allocation and risk mitigation.

Another crucial aspect of risk assessment is understanding the interconnectedness of risks. Often, risks are not isolated phenomena but are interlinked in complex ways. For instance, market downturn can exacerbate credit risks, which might then cascade into operational disruptions. Therefore, assessing risks in a siloed manner can lead to underestimations. Identifying these relationships requires a thorough analysis, often involving systems thinking and network models.

In modern investment landscapes, integrating both qualitative and quantitative assessments is essential. Qualitative assessments leverage human intuition and market experience, providing insights that aren't always quantifiable. Quantitative assessments, on the other hand, utilize data and statistical models to offer measurable and objective evaluations of risk. Balancing both approaches ensures a comprehensive understanding.

Effective risk identification and assessment are not just technical functions; they also require a cultural shift within organizations. Cultivating a risk-aware culture helps in ensuring that risks are acknowledged and addressed promptly. Leaders should encourage open discussions about potential risks and near-misses, making it a routine part of meetings and strategic discussions.

Technology plays a crucial role in assisting risk identification and assessment. Advanced analytical tools, artificial intelligence, and machine learning algorithms can process vast amounts of data to identify patterns and signals of potential risks. For instance, AI-driven analysis can offer early warnings for market shifts, providing an edge in proactive risk management.

Furthermore, external data sources such as economic indicators, geopolitical developments, and sector-specific news need to be continuously monitored. These sources can often provide early warning signals that might impact your investment portfolio. Incorporating this external intelligence is vital in making your risk assessment process comprehensive and robust.

Investors should also pay attention to emerging trends and evolving risks, such as cybersecurity threats in today's digital era. As our financial systems become more interconnected and reliant on technology, the potential for cyber risks escalates. Incorporating assessments for such modern risks ensures that portfolios remain protected in the ever-changing landscape.

Lastly, communication and collaboration between different functional teams—risk management, compliance, investment, and operations—are fundamental. When teams work in silos, critical information might not be shared effectively, leading to gaps in risk identification and assessment. Encouraging cross-functional collaboration enriches the risk management process, ensuring that all bases are covered.

To summarize, **Risk Identification and Assessment** is an indispensable element of the broader risk management strategy. Identifying and thoroughly assessing risks equips investors and financial professionals with the insights needed to protect and grow their portfolios. It combines both art and science, encompassing diverse methodologies to evaluate risks comprehensively. By continuously refining these processes, you'll foster a resilient investment environment that not only withstands, but also thrives in the face of risks.

Risk Response Strategies

These strategies encompass a critical set of actions and techniques aiming to mitigate, transfer, accept, or avoid risk. The way you respond to financial risks is crucial in preserving the integrity and growth of your investments. This sub-section delves into the dynamic approaches to handling various types of investment risks. We won't just look at these strategies theoretically; we'll analyze them practically to demonstrate their effectiveness.

First and foremost, mitigation involves taking steps to reduce the impact or likelihood of the risk. Mitigation strategies include diversifying your investment portfolio, hedging with financial instruments like options and futures, and setting stop-loss orders to limit potential losses. Diversification spreads your investments across various asset classes, industries, or geographies, minimizing the impact of a downturn in any single area. Hedging, on the other hand, acts as insurance, protecting your portfolio from adverse price movements. Employing these strategies effectively can significantly cushion the blows of market volatility.

Transfer of risk is another vital strategy, often achieved through insurance or contractual agreements. For instance, credit default swaps (CDS) can transfer the risk of a bond default from the holder to the insurer. Similarly, futures contracts can transport the risk of price fluctuations to the seller. By transferring risk, you shift the potential financial impact to a third party, providing a safety net for your investments. Essentially, through instruments like CDS and futures, you're redistributing potential financial losses to parties more willing or capable of absorbing them.

The acceptance of risk is a strategy where investors acknowledge that certain risks are inherent and choose to accept them. This approach isn't about being reckless; it's about being realistic. You'll need to evaluate which risks are worth taking because they come with the potential for higher rewards. Seasoned investors might accept market volatility or economic downturns because their long-term investment horizon allows them to ride out the temporary dips. This strategy often relies on a deep understanding of market trends and a strong stomach for market fluctuations.

Avoidance is perhaps the most straightforward yet sometimes the most difficult to implement. This entails steering clear of investments or decisions where the risk level is unacceptably high. Risk avoidance could mean not entering a highly volatile market or avoiding stocks with a history of unpredictable performance. This strategy requires thorough research and a disciplined approach to investing, ensuring that you don't get swayed by the temptation of quick gains that come with high-risk ventures.

Each of these strategies—mitigation, transfer, acceptance, and avoidance—has its place in a robust risk management framework. A balanced approach is often the most effective. For instance, while diversifying your portfolio (mitigation), you might also purchase insurance (transfer) and decide to accept certain market risks for the potential of higher returns. Simultaneously, you'll avoid investments that don't align with your risk tolerance or financial goals.

Implementing these strategies requires not only knowledge but also the tools to analyze, monitor, and adjust your risk management practices continuously. Advanced software solutions can provide real-time data, scenario analysis, and predictive analytics, helping you stay ahead of potential risks. These tools can automate certain aspects of risk management, making it easier to react swiftly to changing market conditions. Moreover, they offer insights that might not be immediately apparent through manual analysis alone.

In terms of practical application, consider a hedge fund manager deciding to mitigate risk through diversification and dynamic hedging. By allocating capital across various asset classes and employing derivatives to protect against downside risk, the fund can achieve a more balanced risk-reward profile. The manager might use stop-loss orders to automatically sell off assets that dip below a certain price, ensuring minimal losses. Such a multi-faceted approach embodies the principles of effective risk response strategies.

Another practical example is the use of stress testing, which involves simulating extreme market conditions to see how your portfolio holds up. This proactive strategy helps you identify potential weaknesses and prepare contingency plans, thereby reducing the element of surprise. Stress testing can reveal vulnerabilities that might go unnoticed in regular market conditions, allowing you to implement targeted risk management measures before actual crises hit. This technique is a cornerstone of advanced risk management and is especially valuable for institutional investors managing large portfolios.

Monitoring and reviewing your risk response strategies is just as crucial as their initial implementation. Financial markets are never static; economic conditions, political landscapes, and market sentiments can shift rapidly. Regularly review and adjust your risk management strategies to ensure they remain effective. This ongoing process involves staying updated with market trends, revisiting your risk tolerance, and being willing to pivot your strategies as needed. In some cases, this might mean rebalancing your portfolio, modifying your hedging tactics, or updating your risk metrics.

Let's not forget the importance of educating yourself and staying informed. Continuous learning and adapting to new risk management methodologies can make a significant difference in how well you navigate financial uncertainties. Attend seminars, read industry reports, and engage with financial communities to stay ahead of emerging risks and innovative strategies. Knowledge is power, especially when it comes to managing risks in an ever-evolving financial landscape.

In conclusion, **Risk Response Strategies** are about striking the right balance between meticulous planning and dynamic adaptation. By employing a combination of mitigation, transfer, acceptance, and avoidance strategies, and continuously reviewing and adjusting your approach, you can protect and grow your investments. Remember, a well-thought-out risk management plan is your best defense against financial uncertainties and your strongest ally in achieving long-term investment success. So, take these strategies to heart, implement them wisely, and watch your portfolio navigate the tumultuous waters of the financial world with confidence and resilience.

Chapter 3:
Risk Tolerance and Investor Profiles

Understanding risk tolerance is a foundational step in the investment journey, serving as a pivotal guidepost for financial planners and investors alike. It's not merely about quantifying how much risk one can financially withstand, but also about gauging the psychological comfort an investor has with potential losses. By assessing risk tolerance through both quantitative and qualitative measures, one can craft investor profiles that truly resonate with individual preferences and life circumstances. These profiles enable a customized approach to risk management, ensuring that investment strategies are aligned with personal objectives and risk appetites. The ultimate goal is to create a balanced portfolio that can weather market volatility while meeting targeted financial milestones. In this chapter, we'll delve into the nuances of risk tolerance and explore how creating detailed investor profiles can lead to more personalized and effective risk management strategies.

Assessing Risk Tolerance

Assessing risk tolerance is a crucial step in the journey of financial planning and investment management. It's like understanding your own navigational chart before setting sail. Risk tolerance quantifies an investor's ability and willingness to endure market volatility, ensuring the voyage remains both planned and predictable despite the financial tempests.

First, let's break down what risk tolerance entails. At its core, risk tolerance is your comfort level with the possibility of losing some or all of your investment in exchange for potential gains. Every investor has a unique combination of financial goals, timelines, and emotional responses to market movements, which all contribute to their overall risk tolerance. Recognizing your own risk tolerance is as fundamental as knowing your budget; it shapes your investment journey, guiding the types of assets you choose and how you respond to market fluctuations.

When assessing risk tolerance, one must consider several factors. The first is investment horizon—the length of time you're willing to commit to your investments. A longer timeframe generally allows for greater risk-taking, as it affords the opportunity to ride out market dips. Conversely, if you're closer to needing your investment capital, a conservative approach may be more suitable. It's like preparing for a long journey; the more time you have, the more supplies and options you can afford to take.

Financial goals play a pivotal role in assessing risk tolerance. If your objective is to grow your wealth substantially over a short period, you might need to accept higher risk levels. However, if preserving capital for retirement or a child's education is the priority, a lower-risk approach may be appropriate. Understanding these goals clearly can help align your risk tolerance with your overall investment strategy.

Another element to consider is your liquidity needs. If you foresee needing access to your funds in the short term, you'll likely have a lower risk tolerance. Higher liquidity needs necessitate a conservative approach, focusing on stable, easily accessible investments. In contrast, if you can afford to tie up your capital in long-term investments, you might be more open to higher risk levels.

The psychological aspect of risk tolerance is equally important. How would you react if your portfolio lost 20% of its value in a market downturn? The emotional response to financial loss varies significantly among individuals and can influence investment decisions. It's crucial to acknowledge and understand your emotional capacity for risk, as it will affect your ability to stick with your investment plan during volatile periods. Think of it as knowing your stress triggers; understanding them helps manage reactions and maintain a composed strategy.

It's also vital to take into account historical market performance and potential scenarios. Reviewing past market data can help set realistic expectations for your investments. While historical performance isn't a guarantee of future results, it provides a framework for understanding potential risks and rewards. This information forms a foundation on which to build your risk tolerance assessment, offering insight into how different investment strategies might perform over time.

Questionnaires and surveys are common tools used to gauge risk tolerance. These assessments typically ask about your investment objectives, time horizon, current financial situation, and responses to hypothetical market scenarios. By analyzing your answers, financial advisors can obtain a structured measure of your risk tolerance. These tools offer a starting point for a more in-depth conversation about your financial goals and strategies.

Once your risk tolerance has been assessed, it can be translated into an appropriate asset allocation strategy. Asset allocation involves spreading investments across various asset classes—such as stocks, bonds, and cash—to match your risk tolerance. A well-tailored asset allocation can optimize returns while minimizing risk, providing a balanced approach to achieving financial goals.

It's important to periodically reassess your risk tolerance. Life circumstances, financial goals, and market conditions can change, affecting your comfort level with risk. Regular reviews ensure that your investment strategy remains aligned with your current risk tolerance. Think of it as a financial health check-up; just as you monitor your physical health, your financial strategy needs regular evaluations.

For financial planners and advisors, understanding a client's risk tolerance is foundational to providing appropriate investment recommendations. It requires effective communication, empathy, and a comprehensive approach to gathering and analyzing information. Building strong client relationships based on trust and mutual understanding enhances the ability to craft personalized investment strategies that reflect each client's unique risk tolerance.

In summary, assessing risk tolerance is not a one-time event but an ongoing process. It involves a deep understanding of financial goals, timelines, emotional responses, and market expectations. By accurately gauging risk tolerance, investors can make informed decisions that align with their comfort levels and long-term objectives. Ultimately, a clear grasp of risk tolerance enhances financial resilience, enabling investors to navigate market fluctuations with confidence and maintain focus on achieving their financial aspirations.

Creating Investor Profiles for Customized Risk Management

This involves more than just a cursory glance at an investor's willingness to take a risk. It's a comprehensive process that requires an intimate understanding of both quantitative metrics and qualitative insights. The fusion of these elements allows financial professionals to tailor risk management strategies that are not only more effective but also more aligned with investor goals and aptitudes.

To start, it's essential to recognize that investor profiles are multifaceted constructs. They're built on key factors such as financial goals, time horizons, risk tolerance, and individual circumstances.

These profiles act as the cornerstone of customized risk management. By understanding an investor's unique context, financial planners can propose strategies that maximize returns while minimizing risk exposure.

One pivotal element in creating investor profiles is assessing financial goals. Objectives range from short-term needs like buying a car or funding a vacation to long-term plans such as retirement or estate planning. Each goal has its own risk-return trade-off, influencing how assets should be allocated. For example, a young investor saving for retirement can afford to take on more risk, whereas someone nearing retirement might prioritize capital preservation.

Time horizon is another critical aspect. The length of time an investor expects to hold an investment significantly impacts the suitability of various risk management strategies. Generally, the longer the time horizon, the higher the risk tolerance, as there's more time to recover from potential losses. Conversely, shorter time horizons typically necessitate a more conservative approach.

Risk tolerance is perhaps the most discussed component, yet it's often misunderstood or oversimplified. Measuring risk tolerance involves both objective assessments—like risk tolerance questionnaires—and subjective evaluations, including interviews and behavioral analysis. Objective tools help quantify risk tolerance, but subjective methods capture nuances that numbers alone can't reveal. This comprehensive approach ensures that the investor profile is complete and accurate.

Additionally, individual circumstances can't be overlooked. Factors such as income, debt levels, family obligations, health, and even job security play roles in defining an individual's risk profile. For instance, a high earner with minimal debt might be able to sustain higher risk levels compared with someone who has a lower income and considerable financial obligations.

Once these variables are meticulously analyzed, the next step involves crafting the customized risk management strategies. These strategies often include asset allocation models, diversification techniques, and specific financial instruments tailored to the investor's profile. For instance, a risk-averse investor may find solace in bonds and low-risk mutual funds, whereas a risk-seeking investor might prefer equities and alternative investments like real estate or commodities.

Moreover, behavioral finance principles are invaluable when creating investor profiles. Understanding how psychological biases—such as loss aversion, overconfidence, and herd behavior—affect decision-making can help tailor more robust strategies. By addressing these biases upfront, financial planners can better prepare investors for market volatility and emotional pitfalls.

Customization goes further into life stage planning. The financial needs and risk appetites of individuals evolve with life events—marriage, childbirth, education funding, and retirement. Regularly updating investor profiles to accommodate these changes is essential for ongoing risk management. It's a dynamic process rather than a one-time setup.

Let's consider the role of continuous education and communication. Educating clients about market principles, risk, and reward helps manage expectations and align them with reality. Transparent and frequent communication builds trust and enables timely adjustments to the investment strategy. Investors who are informed and involved tend to stick to their plans, even in turbulent times, thus reducing panic-driven decisions.

In particular, the integration of technology has transformed the creation and updating of investor profiles. Tools such as robo-advisors and advanced analytics can process vast arrays of data to generate precise risk management strategies. However, while technology offers accuracy and efficiency, it should complement rather than replace the human touch. Personalized advice and the emotional support provided by a financial advisor remain irreplaceable.

A case in point involves using scenario analysis and stress testing within customized risk management plans. These techniques allow investors to understand the potential impacts of various financial shocks, such as market downturns or interest rate changes, on their portfolios. By preparing for these scenarios, investors can make more informed decisions, enhancing their ability to navigate financial uncertainties.

Ultimately, crafting investor profiles for customized risk management is a marriage of art and science. It requires a balance between rigorous analytical processes and a deep understanding of human behavior. Mastering this balance not only safeguards investments against potential risks but also empowers investors to achieve their financial aspirations with confidence and peace of mind.

Creating finely tuned investor profiles is essential for effective risk management. By tailoring strategies to individual needs, time horizons, and risk appetites, financial professionals can build resilient portfolios that stand the test of time and market conditions. Continual learning, open communication, and adaptive strategies ensure that the relationship between investor and advisor thrives, benefiting both parties in the long run.

Chapter 4:
Asset Diversification

Asset diversification is the cornerstone of modern investment strategy, harmonizing risk and reward in an ever-volatile market landscape. By spreading investments across a broader spectrum of asset classes—from equities and bonds to real estate and commodities—investors can mitigate the impact of poor performance in any single asset. This practice not only cushions the portfolio against market swings but also aligns with the foundational principles of risk management. Diversification isn't merely a defensive tactic; it's an active strategy to enhance potential yields through exposure to various growth opportunities. A thoughtful approach to diversification requires constant evaluation and rebalancing, ensuring that your portfolio's risk profile aligns with both market conditions and personal risk tolerance. Ultimately, a well-diversified portfolio not only safeguards against uncertainties but also positions for long-term growth, paving the way for a more resilient financial future.

The Theory and Practice of Diversification

This is one of the foundational principles in risk management, especially crucial within the realm of investment. When we talk about diversification, we're fundamentally addressing how investors can spread their investments to reduce exposure to any single asset or risk. By doing so, they aim to lessen the volatility in their portfolio. The basic idea is simple: don't put all your eggs in one basket. However, the application of this theory is both an art and a science, necessitating a deep understanding of various asset classes, market correlations, and investment strategies.

The theory of diversification hinges on the concept of correlation. Correlation measures the degree to which two assets move in relation to each other. Ideally, a well-diversified portfolio will contain assets that are not perfectly correlated, meaning they don't react in the same way to market movements. For instance, when the stock market declines, bonds often perform better or remain steady. Including both in a portfolio can help smooth returns over time. This idea of mixing uncorrelated assets to manage risk is central to modern portfolio theory (MPT), developed by Harry Markowitz in the 1950s. MPT suggests that an investor can achieve an optimal portfolio that balances risk and return by carefully selecting a mix of investments.

This theory isn't just academic; its practical application has profound effects on investment success. When investors fail to diversify adequately, they expose themselves to unsystematic risk—or the risk that can be mitigated through diversification. On the other hand, no amount of diversification can eliminate systematic risk, which is inherent to the entire market. This differentiation between risks underscores why merely owning a variety of stocks isn't enough; those stocks need to be selected based on their low correlation with each other.

Implementing diversification in practice involves more than just spreading money across various assets. Investors must consider asset class diversification, geographic diversification, sector diversification, and even diversification across investment styles. Asset class diversification means holding different types of investments, such as stocks, bonds, real estate, and commodities. Geographic diversification involves owning assets from different countries or regions to mitigate the impact of local economic downturns. Sector diversification spreads investments across different industries, like technology, healthcare, and finance, while style diversification covers different investment strategies, such as value versus growth investing.

An effective way to achieve diversification is through the use of mutual funds and exchange-traded funds (ETFs). These instruments inherently provide diversification by pooling resources from many investors to buy a broad array of securities. This model allows investors to gain exposure to multiple sectors and assets with a single investment, thereby mitigating individual security risk. However, investors should also be cautious of over-diversification, where the portfolio becomes so diluted that the benefits of diversification are lost and potential returns are diminished.

Asset allocation is a critical component of diversification and involves determining the proportion of the portfolio to be invested in various asset classes. This decision is both art and science, influenced by the investor's risk tolerance, investment horizon, and financial goals. Strategic asset allocation provides a long-term map, while tactical asset allocation allows short-term adjustments based on market conditions. For example, an investor might have a strategic goal to allocate 60% of their portfolio to equities and 40% to bonds. However, based on current market analysis, they might tactically adjust this split to 55% equities and 45% bonds.

Advanced diversification strategies may involve the use of alternative investments like private equity, hedge funds, and commodities. These assets often exhibit different risk-return profiles compared to traditional stocks and bonds, and can thus provide an additional layer of diversification. For example, commodities like gold often perform well during market downturns, providing a hedge against equity market volatility. However, these advanced strategies come with their own risks and complexities, requiring thorough due diligence and a clear understanding of the underlying assets.

Let's consider a real-world example to illustrate the benefits of diversification. During the 2008 financial crisis, investors who had heavily concentrated their portfolios in the financial sector faced substantial losses. Meanwhile, those who had diversified across various sectors—including consumer staples, healthcare, and technology—experienced less dramatic declines and recovered more quickly. This practical case underscores the importance of diversification in protecting one's investment portfolio from sector-specific downturns.

While the benefits of diversification are evident, it's not a set-it-and-forget-it strategy. Regular portfolio rebalancing is crucial to maintain the desired level of diversification. Over time, the performance of different investments will shift the original asset allocation. Without rebalancing, an initially diversified portfolio can become skewed towards more volatile asset classes, increasing risk. Rebalancing involves periodically buying and selling assets to realign the portfolio with its strategic allocation. This discipline ensures that the portfolio stays aligned with the investor's risk tolerance and financial objectives.

In conclusion, **The Theory and Practice of Diversification** should be an indispensable part of every investor's toolkit. It combines the science of correlation and risk management with the art of strategic and tactical asset allocation. By thoughtfully diversifying across asset classes, geographies, sectors, and investment styles, investors can mitigate risk, achieve more stable returns, and build resilient portfolios. However, diversification is not a one-time effort but a continuous process that requires regular review and adjustment to align with changing market conditions and personal financial goals. Remember, the path to financial success is not about avoiding risk altogether but managing it wisely through sound diversification strategies.

Asset Allocation Models

These models are vital in shaping the foundation of effective portfolio management and risk mitigation strategies. They are not just theoretical constructs but tools actively used to balance risk and return, maximizing the potential of an investor's financial journey. Asset allocation's central idea is to spread investments across different asset classes to minimize risks and capitalize on the market's unpredictable nature. However, this concept goes far beyond just creating a diversified portfolio. It's a scientific approach that integrates an investor's risk tolerance, investment goals, and market conditions.

When discussing asset allocation models, one must understand the primary types and theories behind them. There are several popular models, each with its advantages and strategy alignments. Two of the most widely recognized models are Strategic Asset Allocation (SAA) and Tactical Asset Allocation (TAA). While Strategic Asset Allocation is centered around a fixed framework based on long-term market expectations, Tactical Asset Allocation introduces the flexibility to adjust based on short-term opportunities or market conditions.

The Strategic Asset Allocation (SAA) model involves setting a base policy mix—a proportional combination of assets based on expected returns, variance, and correlation of different asset classes. This model is almost like a financial constitution, providing a steady and disciplined approach that prohibits frequent changes in the allocation. Proponents argue that this model exploits the long-term trends and the law of mean reversion, where asset classes tend to return to their historical averages eventually.

Comparatively, Tactical Asset Allocation (TAA) permits short-term deviations from the established baseline allocations to exploit market anomalies or economic conditions. For instance, portfolio managers might shift capital from bonds to stocks if they foresee a bull market. Though TAA introduces a layer of flexibility, it also brings a higher risk due to its speculative nature. However, if executed correctly, it can significantly enhance portfolio performance. Balancing SAA and TAA can provide a robust strategy, enabling portfolios to benefit from long-term trends while seizing short-term opportunities.

Another prominent model worth discussing is the Dynamic Asset Allocation (DAA). Unlike SAA and TAA, which might either adhere strictly or allow tactical shifts, DAA continually adjusts the asset mix in response to changing market conditions. It's flexible and adjusts strategically, making it suitable for navigating volatile markets or economic cycles. Dynamic models consider economic indicators such as interest rates, GDP growth, and geopolitical events, thus offering a responsive approach to market fluctuations.

It's essential to also highlight the benefits and risks associated with Insured Asset Allocation. This model follows a mechanism akin to an insurance policy where a portfolio is managed based on predefined floor values. If the portfolio value drops to these floor levels, risk exposure is minimized to protect against further losses. It's particularly popular in retirement planning, where preserving capital is crucial. While it offers peace of mind, overly conservative adjustments might hinder the capture of potential market upsides. Therefore, it demands astute management to balance protection and growth actively.

Moreover, the concept of Constant-Weighting Asset Allocation brings another perspective. This strategy involves adjusting the portfolio back to its original target allocation at set intervals. Suppose the target is 60% stocks and 40% bonds. If the stocks surpass their target weight due to a market rally, this model mandates selling some of the appreciated stocks and buying bonds to revert to the initial allocation. It's a disciplined approach encouraging the classic buy-low, sell-high strategy. However, portfolio rebalancing can incur transaction costs and tax implications, warranting a careful cost-benefit analysis.

Modern advancements have introduced the Goal-Based Allocation model, which aligns investments with specific financial goals rather than risk profiles alone. This client-centric model segments the portfolio into goal-specific sub-portfolios, each designed to meet particular objectives like buying a home, funding education, or retirement planning. It personalizes the traditional asset allocation approach, emphasizing that individuals have multi-layered financial aspirations needing diverse strategies. Its success hinges on the precise definition of goals and relative return requirements for each, making communication and clarity between investors and financial advisors paramount.

While discussing these models, it's crucial to remember the ideological shift instigated by Behavioral Finance. Traditional asset allocation models are typically grounded in classical economic theories assuming rational decision-making. However, real-world investors often deviate from rationality, influenced by biases and emotions. Behavioral considerations advocate for models incorporating psychological factors, addressing why people might flee from equities during downturns despite long-term growth prospects. Addressing these biases in asset allocation ensures a more tailored and realistic approach, aligning more closely with the investor's natural tendencies.

Furthermore, advances in technology and the advent of robo-advisors have revolutionized asset allocation models. These automated platforms utilize algorithms to construct and adjust portfolios based on modern portfolio theory principles, risk tolerance, and market conditions. They offer cost-effective, efficient, and precise asset allocation solutions. However, the human element remains irreplaceable for nuanced personal insights that algorithms might overlook. The integration of technology and human advisory forms a hybrid model, combining the best of both worlds—efficiency and personalized guidance.

Lastly, Environmental, Social, and Governance (ESG) considerations are increasingly shaping asset allocation decisions. Portfolio managers adopting ESG-based models aim to align investments with ethical values and social responsibility. These models evaluate the sustainability and societal impact of investments, integrating non-financial factors into traditional financial analysis. Research indicates that companies excelling in ESG criteria often exhibit better long-term performance and lower risk profiles, making this approach not just ethically sound but also financially prudent.

In summation, **Asset Allocation Models** transcend mere diversification, encapsulating methodologies that adapt to evolving market dynamics, investor goals, and behavioral tendencies. Whether employing a steadfast model like Strategic Asset Allocation or a more fluid approach such as Dynamic Asset Allocation, the choice hinges upon individual risk tolerance, investment horizon, and financial objectives. As the financial landscape evolves, so must the strategies underpinning portfolio management. By harnessing these models effectively, investors and financial professionals can navigate the complexities of financial markets, achieving a balanced blend of risk and reward.

Chapter 5:
Quantitative Risk Analysis

When it comes to navigating the turbulent waters of financial markets, understanding and implementing quantitative risk analysis is indispensable. This chapter delves into the essential tools and techniques that enable investors and financial professionals to measure and manage risk with precision. By leveraging statistical tools, such as standard deviation, value-at-risk (VaR), and Monte Carlo simulations, one can quantify potential losses and evaluate the probability of adverse outcomes. Moreover, modeling techniques like scenario analysis and stress testing provide a robust framework for predicting how different variables and market conditions might impact an investment portfolio. This blend of rigorous analysis and forward-thinking strategy empowers you to make informed decisions, fine-tune risk management approaches, and ultimately fortify your portfolio against unforeseen challenges. As we venture further into this disciplined approach, remember that a well-executed quantitative analysis not only safeguards assets but also unlocks pathways to seize new opportunities.

Statistical Tools for Risk Identification

Using statistical tools to assess risks serves as the foundation for comprehensively understanding investment risks. These tools are vital for identifying, analyzing, and quantifying the various threats that can impact an investment portfolio. Risk analysts, portfolio managers, and other financial professionals rely heavily on these methods to make informed decisions and protect their investments from potential downturns.

One of the most fundamental statistical tools used for risk identification is *standard deviation*. It measures the dispersion or spread of returns from the mean. By analyzing historical price data, one can determine the volatility of an asset. High standard deviation indicates more variability in returns, which translates to higher risk. On the other hand, a lower standard deviation suggests more stable and predictable asset performance. It's essential for investors to consider standard deviation when assessing the risk level of individual securities and the entire portfolio.

Value at Risk (VaR) is another essential tool. VaR quantifies the maximum potential loss in value over a given time period, at a certain confidence level. Essentially, it asks: "What's the worst-case scenario we can expect within this time frame, with this level of confidence?" For instance, a one-day VaR of $1 million at a 95% confidence level means there is a 5% chance the portfolio could lose more than $1 million in a single day. VaR is widely used in both financial institutions and investment firms to assess the risk of loss and to maintain adequate capital reserves.

Next up is *coefficient of variation (CV)*. This metric is particularly useful when comparing the risk of different investments. The CV is the ratio of an asset's standard deviation to its mean return. It offers a standardized measure of risk per unit of return, making it easier to compare the relative risk of different assets. This tool is instrumental for portfolio managers in the selection and allocation process, as they aim to maximize returns while minimizing risk.

In the context of diversified portfolios, *correlation analysis* plays a crucial role. By examining the correlation coefficients between different assets, investors can understand how assets move in relation to one another. A correlation coefficient ranges from -1 to +1. A value of +1 means that two assets move perfectly in sync, while -1 indicates they move in entirely opposite directions. Ideally, a well-diversified portfolio includes assets that are not highly correlated, reducing overall portfolio risk.

Another powerful statistical method is *regression analysis*. Regression models help identify the relationship between dependent and independent variables, often used to forecast the future behavior of stocks or indexes based on historical data. For instance, a simple linear regression might assess how a particular stock's performance is influenced by an economic indicator like GDP growth. Multiple regression, on the other hand, can include several factors, providing a more comprehensive view of the variables that impact an asset's returns.

Equal in importance is *beta coefficient*, a measure of a stock's volatility relative to the market. A beta of 1 indicates that the stock moves in line with the market. A beta greater than 1 suggests the stock is more volatile than the market, and conversely, a beta of less than 1 implies lower volatility. Understanding an asset's beta allows investors to gauge how market movements might impact a specific security, aiding in portfolio construction and risk management.

Advanced statistical techniques like *Monte Carlo simulations* offer a robust approach to risk identification. By simulating a multitude of possible scenarios, Monte Carlo models can estimate the probability distribution of potential outcomes. This method is immensely beneficial for stress-testing portfolios under various market conditions, providing insights into potential future risks and helping managers prepare more effective risk mitigation strategies.

Expected Shortfall (ES), also known as Conditional VaR (CVaR), is an extension of the VaR concept. While VaR provides the threshold loss, ES offers insights into the tail of the loss distribution. It calculates the average loss that exceeds the VaR threshold, providing a fuller picture of potential extreme losses. This tool is particularly valuable for managing risks in financial crises, where understanding tail risks becomes paramount.

In addition to these classical methods, modern risk analysts often employ *machine learning algorithms*. These algorithms can process vast amounts of data and identify intricate patterns that traditional statistical methods might miss. Techniques such as clustering, classification, and regression trees are increasingly applied to detect emerging risks and refine predictive models. By leveraging the power of machine learning, financial professionals can stay ahead of potential threats and make more informed investment decisions.

Time series analysis is also indispensable for risk identification, where data points are ordered in time. Techniques like Autoregressive Integrated Moving Average (ARIMA) models help predict future values based on past trends. Time series analysis is particularly important for forecasting stock prices, interest rates, and economic indicators, allowing investors to anticipate market movements and adjust their strategies accordingly.

Another intricately related tool is the *credit risk modeling*. For investors dealing with debt instruments, understanding the credit risk of issuers is crucial. Models such as the Merton model, which uses options pricing theory to assess credit risk, are commonly employed. These models can forecast the probability of default and loss given default, providing insights necessary for managing credit exposure effectively.

Scenario analysis and *stress testing* are also pivotal in capturing risks that might not be evident through historical data alone. By envisioning various hypothetical scenarios—ranging from economic downturns to geopolitical events—investors can evaluate the potential impact on their portfolios. Stress testing, in particular, pushes models to the limits to understand how portfolios would perform under extreme but plausible conditions. This proactive approach helps in building resilient portfolios capable of weathering unexpected shocks.

Dependencies and relationships among variables in more complex settings can be identified using *copula models*. These models help in understanding the joint distribution of multiple assets and the dependence structure between them. They are particularly useful in evaluating the risk of portfolios containing diverse asset classes, as they provide a more nuanced view of potential co-movements and joint extreme events than simple correlation measures.

Lastly, the field of *risk metrics and key performance indicators (KPIs)* serves as the backbone for continuous risk monitoring and identification. Metrics such as Sharpe ratio, Treynor ratio, and Jensen's alpha measure an investment's performance relative to its risk, providing a holistic view of risk-adjusted returns. KPIs are also indispensable for decision-making processes, helping investors and managers to track performance, detect anomalies, and take corrective action promptly.

Sharpe ratio, in particular, quantifies risk-adjusted return by dividing the excess return of an asset by its standard deviation. This metric allows investors to understand how well an investment compensates for the risk taken, aiding in the evaluation and comparison of various assets. A higher Sharpe ratio indicates better risk-adjusted performance, making it an invaluable tool in portfolio management.

By integrating these statistical tools,

Modeling Techniques and Scenario Analysis

These are crucial tools in quantitative risk analysis, driving deeper insights into potential risk exposures and guiding informed decision-making. These methodologies equip financial professionals with the ability to project and plan for an array of future uncertainties, ensuring robust and resilient investment strategies.

One of the foundational modeling techniques is the Monte Carlo simulation, a method that leverages randomness to model the probability of different outcomes in a process that cannot easily be predicted due to the intervention of random variables. Investors and portfolio managers use this technique to simulate market behavior, forecast portfolio performance, and assess the probability of achieving financial goals. By running thousands or even millions of simulations, professionals can generate a probability distribution of possible outcomes, providing a more comprehensive understanding of potential risks and returns.

Another influential model is Value at Risk (VaR), which estimates the maximum potential loss of an investment portfolio over a specified time frame and at a given confidence level. For example, a 1-day VaR at 95% confidence level might show the maximum expected loss one could incur in a day, considering normal market conditions. VaR is particularly favored due to its simplicity and universal applicability. However, it's not without limitations, as it doesn't account for extreme market moves outside the confidence interval, necessitating the use of complementary techniques.

Conditional Value at Risk (CVaR), also known as Expected Shortfall, addresses some of VaR's limitations by considering the tail risk of the loss distribution. While VaR might indicate a maximum threshold of loss, CVaR focuses on the average loss beyond this threshold, giving a clearer picture of potential heavy losses. This makes CVaR a valuable tool for stress testing portfolios under adverse market conditions, enhancing a firm's risk management framework.

Scenario analysis, often employed alongside these modeling techniques, involves evaluating the impact of extraordinary but plausible events on investment portfolios. This could include historical events, such as the 2008 financial crisis, or hypothetical situations like geopolitical upheavals or natural disasters. Financial planners and risk analysts can create bespoke scenarios tailored to their portfolio specifics, dissecting potential impacts and preparing contingency plans accordingly.

Stress testing, which is a subset of scenario analysis, pushes this concept further by applying extreme conditions to models. Unlike routine market fluctuations considered by VaR or Monte Carlo, stress testing places portfolios under 'worst-case' scenarios. This might include catastrophic events such as sudden market crashes, regulatory changes, or significant credit defaults. Stress tests serve as an acid test for the resilience of an investment strategy, highlighting vulnerabilities that might not surface under typical conditions. The insights gained from these tests can be pivotal for recalibrating risk appetite and ensuring robust risk mitigation strategies.

Beyond individual techniques, integrated risk management approaches like RiskMetrics bring a comprehensive perspective. This framework consolidates various risk measures, combining historical data, statistical measures, and forward-looking estimates to provide a holistic risk assessment. By bringing disparate risk measures under one roof, integrated approaches foster better decision-making and ensure alignment with broader business objectives.

Navigating these modeling techniques requires a balance of theoretical knowledge and practical application. Real-world financial data is often imperfect and messy, necessitating strong analytical prowess and the ability to discern signal from noise. Advanced financial professionals use sophisticated software to perform these analyses, including tools like MATLAB, R, SAS, and Python, which offer a range of libraries and packages for financial modeling and quantitative analysis. The choice of tool often depends on the specific requirements and complexity of the analysis, as well as the professional's familiarity with the software.

For instance, Python's pandas and NumPy libraries, combined with statistical tools like SciPy and visualization packages such as Matplotlib, offer a powerful ecosystem for performing detailed financial analyses and creating informative visuals. These tools facilitate a seamless workflow from data importation, manipulation, analysis, to visualization, ensuring that risk insights are not only accurate but also effectively communicated to stakeholders.

It's also valuable to integrate these modeling techniques within a broader risk governance framework. Effective risk management isn't just about identifying and quantifying risks; it's about embedding these processes into the decision-making fabric of the organization. This involves setting clear risk policies, defining risk tolerances, and ensuring ongoing monitoring and reporting. By operationalizing risk management, organizations can create a risk-aware culture that proactively addresses potential issues before they escalate.

Model validation plays a critical role in this framework. Financial models are based on assumptions and simplifications of reality, which means they need regular scrutiny to ensure their accuracy and relevance. Model validation involves back-testing against historical data, cross-validation with alternative models, and sensitivity analysis to assess how changes in inputs affect outputs. This rigorous process helps identify potential model risks and ensures the models' robustness against a range of scenarios.

Furthermore, continuous learning and development are essential for professionals using these techniques. The financial landscape is constantly evolving, with new risks and opportunities emerging regularly. As such, staying updated with the latest advancements in risk modeling, attending industry conferences, participating in professional development programs, and engaging with academic research are crucial for maintaining a competitive edge.

In summary, **Modeling Techniques and Scenario Analysis** form the bedrock of quantitative risk management, offering invaluable insights for safeguarding investment portfolios. By leveraging a mix of Monte Carlo simulations, VaR, CVaR, and stress testing, alongside scenario analysis, financial professionals can navigate uncertainties with greater confidence. Integrating these methodologies within a robust risk governance framework ensures that risk management is not just reactive but proactive, fostering a resilient and forward-looking approach to financial decision-making.

Chapter 6:
Qualitative Risk Considerations

In this chapter, we dive into the qualitative aspects of risk considerations, aiming to enrich your understanding beyond the numbers and charts. While quantitative methods are fundamental, they don't tell the whole story. Qualitative risk considerations involve understanding behavioral biases and their impact on risk perception, something that's equally crucial for making well-rounded investment decisions. Think of it as reading between the lines of the data—you've got to grasp not only the cold, hard statistics but also the softer, subtler human factors that influence market dynamics. You'll find that incorporating qualitative methods, like expert judgment and scenario analysis, into your risk assessment toolkit can provide a more comprehensive view of potential risks and opportunities. This holistic approach not only empowers you to foresee possible pitfalls but also helps you craft strategies that align closely with the inherently human elements of the marketplace. Understand this blend, and you'll take your risk management game to an entirely new level, achieving both precision and depth in your investment decisions.

Behavioral Biases and Risk Perception

Biases and risk perception play a critical role in investment decision-making, often without investors even realizing it. While traditional finance assumes that individuals act rationally and make decisions based solely on available information, behavioral finance acknowledges that psychological biases and emotions influence humans.

Understanding these biases is crucial for investors, financial planners, and risk management professionals alike. By recognizing how these biases affect risk perception, one can better navigate the complexities of financial markets and optimize investment strategies.

One of the most pervasive behavioral biases is overconfidence. Investors often overestimate their ability to predict market movements or the performance of specific assets, leading to excessive risk-taking. This overconfidence can result in under-diversified portfolios, as investors may place too much trust in their stock-picking skills. To mitigate this, it's important to regularly re-evaluate your investment decisions and seek external opinions. Additionally, utilizing quantitative analysis and scenario planning can help ground your investment strategy in objective data rather than subjective confidence.

Another significant bias is loss aversion. Studies have shown that people tend to prefer avoiding losses rather than acquiring equivalent gains—essentially, the pain of losing is psychologically more impactful than the joy of winning. Loss aversion can lead to overly conservative investment choices, causing individuals to miss out on potential gains. Investors may hold onto losing stocks longer than they should, hoping these stocks will bounce back, thereby worsening their financial position. Setting predetermined stop-loss levels and adhering strictly to them can help circumvent the pitfalls of loss aversion.

Anchoring is another cognitive bias that can distort risk perception. This occurs when individuals rely too heavily on the first piece of information they receive (the "anchor") when making decisions. For instance, an investor might fixate on a stock's historical high price and assume it will return to that level, despite new market conditions or changes in the company's fundamentals. Diversifying information sources and continuously updating your assessments based on the most recent data can counteract the anchor effect.

The herd mentality, or the bandwagon effect, profoundly influences risk perception as well. During market rallies or downturns, investors often mimic the actions of the crowd, assuming the collective wisdom must be correct. However, following the crowd can lead to inflated asset prices during bubbles and excessive pessimism during market crashes. It's essential to conduct independent research and develop a personalized investment strategy that aligns with your risk tolerance and financial goals, instead of succumbing to the pressure of popular opinion.

Confirmation bias further complicates rational decision-making. This bias involves the tendency to search for, interpret, and remember information in a way that confirms one's preconceptions. Thus, investors might selectively gather information that supports their existing beliefs and disregard data that contradicts them. To overcome confirmation bias, consider actively seeking out information and opinions that challenge your views. Employing a contrarian perspective can also reveal opportunities that others may overlook.

Further complicating investment decisions is the recency bias, where investors give undue importance to the most recent events over long-term historical data. This can result in hasty decisions based on short-term market movements. To mitigate this bias, it's important to adopt a long-term investment horizon and focus on fundamentals rather than getting swayed by recent volatility. Creating a well-researched investment plan and sticking to it can help buffer the effects of recency bias.

A comprehensive understanding of these behavioral biases and their impact on risk perception is not just academic; it has real-world implications. Financial planners and portfolio managers who acknowledge and address these biases are better equipped to guide their clients towards more balanced and rational investment decisions. An investor who is aware of their own biases can take steps to mitigate their effects, such as diversifying their portfolio, employing rigorous risk assessment methods, and maintaining discipline in their investment strategies.

Training and education in behavioral finance can also play a pivotal role. By learning about common cognitive biases and their implications on risk perception, finance professionals can enhance their ability to manage clients' portfolios effectively. This education might include formal coursework, attending seminars, or reading recent research in the field. Continuous learning and professional development in behavioral finance are key to staying ahead in the ever-evolving financial landscape.

Incorporating behavioral insights into risk management frameworks can also enhance their efficacy. For instance, financial institutions might incorporate behavioral triggers in their risk models to better predict and mitigate crises. By understanding the psychological factors that drive market participants, these models can become more robust and resilient to unforeseen shocks.

Motivationally, recognizing and countering behavioral biases can empower investors and finance professionals to take control of their financial futures. It's not just about identifying the biases but also about actively instituting processes and disciplines to overcome them. This proactive approach can lead to more consistent investment performance and better adherence to long-term financial goals. Remember, awareness is the first step towards overcoming the pitfalls of behavioral biases.

In inspirational terms, the journey toward mastering behavioral biases and risk perception is a path to becoming a more resilient and informed investor. It's about evolving from a position of unconscious bias to one of deliberate and thoughtful decision-making. By continuously striving to understand the psychological factors influencing your investment choices, you take a significant step towards achieving true financial wisdom and success.

In conclusion, **Behavioral Biases and Risk Perception** are deeply intertwined elements that shape financial decisions in profound ways. Awareness and understanding of biases such as overconfidence, loss aversion, anchoring, herd mentality, confirmation bias, and recency bias can help in developing more rational investment strategies. By leveraging educational resources, incorporating behavioral insights into risk management models, and maintaining a disciplined approach, investors and financial professionals can significantly enhance their ability to manage risk and achieve financial success. Remember, mastering these aspects is not merely an academic exercise but a practical tool for navigating the complexities of the financial markets.

Qualitative Risk Assessment Methods

These form a cornerstone of comprehensive risk management, providing valuable insights that go beyond numerical analysis. While quantitative methods employ mathematical models to predict and measure risk, qualitative approaches delve into the more nuanced aspects of risk, capturing elements that are often overlooked in statistical data. Investors, financial planners, and risk analysts can benefit significantly from integrating these methods into their risk assessment toolkits.

One of the primary qualitative methods is expert judgment. This involves consulting with individuals who have extensive experience and expertise in a specific field. Their insights can illuminate potential risks that may not be immediately apparent through quantitative analysis alone. For instance, an industry veteran might foresee geopolitical issues affecting international investments where statistical models only consider historical financial data. Expert judgment is particularly useful when dealing with unprecedented or emerging risks, where historical data may be scarce or non-existent.

Another key method is the Delphi technique. This structured communication approach involves a panel of experts who anonymously contribute their opinions on potential risks. Through multiple rounds of questioning and feedback, a consensus is reached. This iterative process helps filter out individual biases and achieves a more balanced risk assessment. The Delphi method is especially valuable for gauging risk in complex scenarios where multiple variables and uncertainties intertwine.

Focus groups and workshops also play a crucial role. These settings encourage diverse stakeholders to discuss potential risks in a collaborative environment. Such discussions can unearth risks that quantitative models might miss. For example, employees across different levels of an organization may identify operational risks that aren't reflected in financial models. The collaborative nature of these sessions fosters a comprehensive understanding of the risks involved and promotes a culture of risk awareness within the organization.

Scenario planning stands out as another powerful qualitative tool. This method involves crafting detailed narratives about possible future events and how they might impact investments or business operations. Instead of providing a single predicted outcome, scenario planning encourages consideration of various possibilities, each with its own set of risks and opportunities. For instance, a company might develop scenarios around potential regulatory changes or shifts in consumer behavior. This approach allows for greater flexibility and preparedness in the face of uncertainty.

In addition to these methods, SWOT analysis (Strengths, Weaknesses, Opportunities, Threats) offers a straightforward yet effective framework for risk assessment. By systematically examining these four dimensions, investors and portfolio managers can gain a clearer perspective on where risks and opportunities lie. For example, an asset manager might use SWOT analysis to assess the potential impact of market volatility on a diversified portfolio, identifying both the vulnerabilities and the areas of potential growth.

Moreover, risk workshops can be instrumental in bringing qualitative risk assessment to life. These workshops gather key stakeholders to discuss and brainstorm potential risks and their implications. Through structured exercises and open dialogue, participants can explore a wide range of risks and assess their potential impact. This participatory approach not only enhances risk identification but also fosters a culture of risk management within the organization.

Interviewing is another indispensable qualitative method. By conducting in-depth interviews with key individuals, such as senior management, customers, or industry experts, you can gather nuanced insights into potential risks. These conversations often reveal valuable information that might not surface through surveys or quantitative data analysis. For example, a series of interviews with supply chain managers might uncover potential disruptions that weren't previously considered.

Brainstorming sessions offer a more informal but highly effective way to identify risks. Bringing together a diverse group of individuals to generate ideas about potential risks can lead to unexpected and valuable insights. This method leverages the collective creativity and knowledge of the participants, often resulting in the identification of risks that might not be apparent through more structured methods.

Stakeholder analysis also deserves attention. This method involves identifying and analyzing the interests and influences of various stakeholders in relation to potential risks. By understanding the perspectives of different stakeholders, such as customers, suppliers, regulators, and employees, you can gain a more comprehensive view of the risks involved. For instance, stakeholder analysis could help identify reputational risks that might arise from a new business initiative.

Root cause analysis, although often associated with problem-solving, is also valuable for qualitative risk assessment. This method involves investigating the underlying causes of potential risks, rather than just addressing their symptoms. By identifying root causes, you can develop more effective strategies for mitigating risks. For example, instead of simply addressing a decline in product quality, root cause analysis might reveal underlying issues in the manufacturing process that need to be rectified to prevent future risks.

Qualitative risk assessment is not just about identifying risks but also about understanding their context and impact. The context in which risks occur can significantly influence their severity and likelihood. For instance, a political risk in a stable country might be less concerning than the same risk in a volatile region. Understanding the broader context helps in prioritizing risks and developing appropriate mitigation strategies.

The significance of qualitative methods is further amplified in assessing strategic risks. Unlike operational or financial risks, strategic risks are often tied to an organization's long-term goals and objectives. They're harder to quantify but can have profound implications for the organization's future. Through qualitative assessment, you can identify potential strategic risks, such as changes in competitive dynamics, technological disruptions, or shifts in customer preferences, and develop proactive strategies to address them.

When it comes to behavioral biases, qualitative assessments are particularly adept at uncovering how human emotions and cognitive biases influence risk perception and decision-making. Understanding these biases, such as overconfidence, herd behavior, or aversion to loss, can help investors and financial planners make more rational and objective decisions. For instance, by recognizing a tendency towards overconfidence, an investor can take steps to ensure a more balanced and diversified approach.

Integrating qualitative and quantitative risk assessment methods offers a holistic approach to risk management. While quantitative methods provide the empirical foundation, qualitative methods add depth and context, capturing aspects that numbers alone cannot. This integrated approach ensures a more comprehensive understanding of risks, leading to better-informed decisions. For example, combining statistical models with expert judgment and scenario planning can provide a more robust assessment of market risks and opportunities.

Ultimately, the power of qualitative risk assessment lies in its ability to provide a richer, more nuanced understanding of potential risks. By embracing a range of qualitative methods, investors, financial planners, and risk analysts can uncover hidden risks, explore complex scenarios, and develop more effective strategies for mitigating risks. In an ever-changing and uncertain world, the ability to see beyond the numbers and understand the broader context of risks is an invaluable skill that can make all the difference in protecting and growing investment portfolios.

By effectively integrating qualitative risk assessment methods into your risk management processes, you can enhance your ability to anticipate, identify, and mitigate risks. This proactive approach not only safeguards your investments but also positions you to seize opportunities in an increasingly complex financial landscape. So, take the time to explore and implement these qualitative methods, and you'll be well-equipped to navigate the uncertainties and challenges that lie ahead.

Chapter 7:
Market Risk and Volatility

Understanding market risk and volatility is essential for navigating the financial landscape with confidence and resilience. Market risk, often driven by macroeconomic factors, geopolitical events, and market sentiment, can cause significant fluctuations in the value of investment portfolios. It's crucial to measure this risk using tools like Value at Risk (VaR) and stress testing, enabling us to anticipate potential losses. While we can't eliminate market risk, we can implement hedging strategies, such as options and futures, to mitigate its impact. Recognizing and responding to volatility not only protects our assets but also positions us to capitalize on opportunities arising from market movements. Ultimately, mastering market risk management fosters a proactive and informed investment approach, empowering us to achieve our financial goals amidst an ever-changing economic environment.

Understanding and Measuring Market Risk

This is crucial for any finance professional aiming to strengthen their investment portfolio. At its core, market risk refers to the possibility of an investor experiencing losses due to factors that affect the overall performance of the financial markets. This encompasses fluctuations in stock prices, interest rates, currency exchange rates, and commodity prices. Unlike specific risks tied to individual assets or industries, market risk is systemic and affects the entire market ecosystem. A thorough grasp of market risk helps in formulating strategies that safeguard investments against unpredictable market fluctuations.

Market risk is typically divided into four primary categories: equity risk, interest rate risk, currency risk, and commodity risk. *Equity risk,* for instance, involves the volatility in stock prices due to market conditions or investor sentiment. Equity risk is prevalent in stock exchanges worldwide and directly impacts shareholders' wealth. By understanding such risk, investors and portfolio managers can adopt strategies like diversification or hedging to buffer against potential market downturns.

Interest rate risk is another critical component of market risk. This involves the uncertainty surrounding future movements in interest rates which can profoundly impact bond prices, loan interest rates, and even equity values. When interest rates rise, the cost of borrowing increases, which can dampen consumer spending and impact corporate profits. Conversely, falling interest rates can boost borrowing and spending but may signal underlying economic weaknesses. Proactively managing this risk involves techniques such as duration analysis and interest rate swaps.

Currency risk, or exchange rate risk, affects investors dealing with international portfolios. Fluctuations in currency values can lead to unexpected gains or losses when converting foreign investments back to the home currency. For instance, an American investor may face a significant impact on the returns of a European investment due to the changing relationship between the U.S. dollar and the euro. To measure and mitigate currency risk, tools like forward contracts and options can be highly effective.

Commodity risk refers to the potential losses due to changing prices of raw materials like oil, gold, or agricultural products. Commodity prices can be extremely volatile due to factors such as geopolitical tensions, natural disasters, and supply chain disruptions. Investors exposed to these markets need to stay informed about global trends and possibly use futures contracts to lock in prices and manage this volatility.

Measuring market risk involves various quantitative techniques and metrics. One of the most widely-used metrics is Value at Risk (VaR). VaR estimates the potential loss in value of a portfolio over a defined period for a given confidence interval. Essentially, it's a statistical technique used to quantify the level of financial risk within a firm or an investment portfolio over a specific time frame. While VaR is not without its limitations, it provides a standardized way to compare risk across different assets or portfolios.

Another critical measure is Conditional Value at Risk (CVaR). Unlike VaR, which provides a threshold value, CVaR estimates the expected loss beyond that threshold. This makes CVaR particularly useful for understanding the tail risk - the risk of extreme losses that occur less frequently but can be catastrophic. By considering both VaR and CVaR, investors can get a more holistic view of the potential risks in their portfolios.

Beta, a measure of an asset's volatility in relation to the market, is also instrumental in understanding market risk. A beta greater than one indicates that the asset is more volatile than the market, whereas a beta less than one signifies lower volatility. Investors use beta to gauge an asset's riskiness relative to the broader market, assisting in portfolio construction that aligns with their risk tolerance.

Stress testing and scenario analysis further refine the understanding of market risk. Stress tests involve simulating extreme market conditions to see how a portfolio would perform under such circumstances. This provides insights into vulnerabilities that may not be apparent in normal market conditions. Scenario analysis, on the other hand, evaluates the impact of specific hypothetical events, such as economic recessions or significant geopolitical developments. These techniques help anticipate and plan for potential adverse outcomes, enhancing the resilience of investment strategies.

Quantitative methods like Monte Carlo simulations also play a pivotal role. These simulations use random sampling and statistical modeling to estimate the probability of different outcomes under various market conditions. By running thousands of simulations, investors can understand the range of possible returns and risks for their portfolios. Monte Carlo simulations are particularly valuable for long-term investment planning, taking into account the compounding effects of risk and return over time.

It's not just about the numbers. Qualitative factors such as economic indicators, market sentiment, and geopolitical events must also be considered. For instance, analyzing central bank policies can offer insights into future interest rate movements, while understanding geopolitical tensions can help anticipate commodity price volatility. Integrating these qualitative aspects with quantitative measures provides a more comprehensive risk assessment.

Effective risk management also involves adopting appropriate risk mitigation strategies. Diversification remains a fundamental strategy, spreading investments across different asset classes to reduce exposure to any single market risk. Other strategies like hedging with derivatives, such as options and futures, can provide essential protection against adverse market movements. Continuous monitoring and rebalancing of the portfolio are essential to ensure that the risk levels remain within acceptable limits.

Understanding and measuring market risk is an ongoing process. Markets are dynamic and constantly evolving, influenced by a multitude of factors. Staying informed, using sophisticated risk measurement tools, and being prepared to adapt strategies are essential steps to safeguard investments and achieve long-term financial goals. By mastering market risk, finance professionals can better navigate through uncertainty, seize opportunities, and create resilient portfolios.

Ultimately, a deep understanding of market risk empowers investors and financial professionals to make more informed decisions. It provides the foundation upon which robust risk management strategies are built, ensuring that portfolios are better prepared to withstand the uncertainties of the market. It's a journey of continuous learning, analysis, and adaptation, requiring both technical expertise and intuitive insight to succeed in a complex financial landscape.

Hedging Strategies and Instruments

These serve as fundamental tools in managing market risk and volatility. Effective hedging can safeguard an investment portfolio against unpredictable market movements, enabling you to maintain a more stable financial standing even in turbulent times. Let's dive into how hedging strategies work and explore various instruments available to mitigate risk.

The essence of hedging lies in taking an offsetting position to balance potential losses in an investment. For instance, if you've invested heavily in equities, you might consider hedging against market downturns by using derivatives such as options or futures. These instruments allow you to lock in prices or create scenarios that counteract negative market movements.

One of the primary hedging instruments is the *option*. An option gives the holder the right, but not the obligation, to buy or sell an asset at a predetermined price within a specific timeframe. There are two types: call options (which give the right to buy) and put options (which give the right to sell). By purchasing put options, investors can protect their portfolios from a drop in asset prices, as these options increase in value when the underlying asset's price decreases.

Futures contracts are another powerful hedging tool. Unlike options, futures obligate the parties to buy or sell the asset at a predetermined future date and price. These are predominantly used by businesses to hedge against price changes in inputs such as commodities. For instance, an airline might use futures contracts to stabilize fuel costs, thus shielding itself from sudden spikes in oil prices.

The strategy of using *swaps* has also become popular. In a typical swap agreement, two parties exchange cash flows or other financial instruments to guard against fluctuations in currency exchange rates or interest rates. Interest rate swaps are commonly used to convert floating-rate debt to fixed-rate debt, thereby providing more predictable financial outgoings.

Hedging isn't only about selecting the right instruments; timing and precision in execution matter significantly. For example, managing the delta in options trading—known as "delta hedging"—requires adjusting your position as the price of the underlying asset changes. This continuous adjustment reduces the risk of an adverse move, although it often involves more sophisticated financial models and tools.

Besides traditional derivatives, *exchange-traded funds (ETFs)* offer innovative ways to hedge. Specific ETFs track indexes that move inversely to particular market sectors. By investing in inverse ETFs, you can gain when the market drops, which serves as an efficient hedging mechanism, especially for smaller investors who might not have direct access to complex instruments like options or futures.

Another versatile hedging strategy is known as *pairs trading*. Here, you simultaneously go long on one asset while shorting another. The aim is to profit from the relative difference in their performances rather than their absolute movements. This can be particularly useful in markets where specific sectors or companies are expected to outperform or underperform relative to their peers.

In corporate finance, *natural hedging* is often used as a risk management technique. This involves structuring operational strategies to reduce exposure, such as matching revenue and cost currencies. For example, a company earning revenues in euros but incurring costs in USD might naturally hedge by making expenditures in euros where possible. It provides a built-in form of risk management without entering into external contracts.

Let's not overlook the role of insurance as a hedging instrument. While not as dynamic as derivatives, insurance can help mitigate specific risks such as property damage or business interruption. Companies often purchase policies covering potential losses from natural disasters or other operational risks, thereby providing a financial safeguard that complements other hedging strategies.

Implementing a *correlation hedge* is another sophisticated approach. This involves constructing a portfolio of assets whose price movements are negatively correlated. Ideally, when one asset's price falls, the other rises, balancing out the overall portfolio performance. Such hedging requires keen market insights and thorough analytical methods.

Considering all these strategies, it is crucial to recognize that each instrument and method has costs associated with it, which can erode returns if not managed properly. Utilizing hedging strategies imposes transactional costs, opportunity costs, and sometimes even liquidity constraints. Therefore, a cost-benefit analysis is indispensable in deciding the extent and nature of hedging required.

Finally, successful hedging isn't just about eradicating risk but optimizing it. Risk cannot be entirely eliminated, but it can be managed in a way that aligns with your financial goals and risk tolerance levels. A well-hedged portfolio allows you to take calculated risks, thereby enabling growth without exposing your investments to debilitating losses.

In conclusion, hedging strategies and instruments can appear complex, but they are vital tools for managing investment risk effectively. By integrating various techniques—from options and futures to swaps and natural hedging—you can construct a resilient portfolio. Understanding the nuances of each instrument allows you to better navigate market volatility, ultimately achieving a balanced and secure financial future.

Chapter 8:
Credit Risk and
Counterparty Exposure

Chapter 8 delves into the critical aspects of credit risk and counterparty exposure—key concerns for anyone tasked with protecting and growing investments. Credit risk refers to the possibility that a borrower or counterparty won't meet their obligations, leading to financial losses. This chapter aims to equip you with strategies for identifying and managing these risks proactively. We'll explore the importance of conducting thorough credit assessments and discuss various methods to mitigate the potential fallout from counterparty defaults. Knowing how to navigate the complexities of credit risk isn't just about safeguarding against losses; it's about seizing new opportunities by understanding the intricate balance between risk and reward. This chapter will arm you with the tools and insights necessary to make informed decisions that can shield your investments from unforeseen credit events, maximizing long-term returns.

Identifying Credit Risk

Identifying and understanding credit risk is a fundamental aspect of financial risk assessment. It's essential to deeply understand what credit risk entails and how it manifests to manage and mitigate it effectively. At its core, credit risk is the possibility that a borrower will fail to meet its obligations in accordance with agreed terms. This failure can have devastating impacts on a lender's financial health, potentially leading to significant monetary losses.

The importance of identifying credit risk cannot be overstated. Imagine the cascading effects of bad credit decisions: defaults lead to financial strain on lenders, which subsequently affects their ability to lend further, rippling through the economy. For investors, misidentifying or underestimating credit risk can erase substantial portions of a portfolio's value, undermining financial goals and eroding trust in the markets.

First, let's consider the primary sources of credit risk. These can be broadly categorized into borrower-specific factors and broader economic or sectoral factors. Borrower-specific factors often include credit history, debt levels, income stability, and the borrower's assets. For instance, a borrower with a mixed or poor credit history represents a higher credit risk than one with a strong track record of timely payments and responsible debt management.

On the other hand, broader economic conditions can influence credit risk substantially. Economic recessions, rising unemployment rates, and sector-specific downturns can increase the likelihood of defaults. Borrowers operating in industries facing economic headwinds, such as the retail or energy sectors during downturns, might pose higher risks to their creditors.

To identify credit risk effectively, financial professionals often rely on various tools and methodologies. One widely used approach is credit scoring models, which use statistical techniques to assess a borrower's creditworthiness. These models consider numerous variables such as payment history, outstanding debt, and the length of credit history, giving lenders a quantitative assessment of risk.

The altitudinous role of credit rating agencies also comes into play. These agencies, including Moody's, S&P Global, and Fitch Ratings, evaluate the creditworthiness of entities ranging from corporations to sovereign nations. Their ratings range from high-grade, indicating lower credit risk, to junk-grade, indicating higher risk. While not foolproof, credit ratings provide a standardized measure to compare different credit risks.

However, solely relying on external ratings and credit scoring models can be dangerous. The financial crisis of 2008 exposed severe inadequacies in these ratings, with numerous highly rated instruments defaulting. Hence, undertaking thorough due diligence is indispensable. This involves delving into the borrower's financial statements, understanding their revenue model, scrutinizing cash flow stability, and evaluating their debt service coverage ratio (DSCR).

Another critical aspect of identifying credit risk is understanding counterparty exposure. For instance, in derivative transactions, the risk isn't just about the underlying asset's performance but also about the counterparty's ability to fulfill their contractual commitments. This makes assessing the creditworthiness of counterparties a pivotal part of credit risk management.

Advanced metrics and ratios also aid in identifying credit risk. The loan-to-value (LTV) ratio, a widely used measure in mortgage lending, compares the loan amount to the property's appraised value. A lower LTV ratio implies lesser credit risk as the borrower has more 'skin in the game'. Similarly, the interest coverage ratio measures a firm's ability to meet its interest obligations from its earnings. Higher ratios signal lower credit risk as they indicate stronger earnings relative to debt obligations.

Economic indicators provide additional insight into credit risk. Factors like GDP growth rates, inflation rates, and central bank policies can significantly affect borrowers' ability to repay. For instance, high inflation can erode purchasing power and increase costs, making it harder for businesses and individuals to service their debts.

Central to these indicators are interest rates. Rising interest rates increase borrowing costs, often leading to higher default rates, particularly for variable-rate loans.

Furthermore, geographical diversification can mitigate credit risk. Spreading credit exposure across various regions can reduce the impact of localized economic downturns. For instance, lending across different states or countries can be a safeguard against regional recessions that might otherwise significantly affect a lender's portfolio.

Technology advancements also play a significant role in identifying credit risk. Big data analytics and machine learning algorithms can analyze vast datasets to detect patterns and predict creditworthiness with higher accuracy. These technologies can process non-traditional data sources, such as social media activity, to supplement traditional credit assessment methods. This holistic approach offers a more comprehensive view of a borrower's risk profile.

However, technology is just a tool. The human element—critical thinking, intuition, and experience—is irreplaceable. Financial institutions benefit immensely from risk analysts and portfolio managers who bring years of expertise to the table. While algorithms might flag potential risks, human oversight ensures these signals are interpreted correctly and in context.

Regulatory frameworks also impact how credit risk is identified and managed. Regulations mandate specific practices and disclosures which enhance transparency and reduce information asymmetry. For instance, the Basel III framework requires banks to maintain higher capital buffers to absorb potential losses, promoting stability in the banking sector. Compliance with such regulations ensures that credit risk is meticulously assessed and managed.

Staying informed about industry developments is equally crucial. Continuous education on new regulations, emerging risks, and advancements in risk assessment methodologies is vital for financial professionals. Participating in industry conferences, enrolling in advanced courses, and engaging in peer discussions can significantly enhance one's ability to identify and manage credit risk.

Collaboration within and across industries can provide deeper insights into credit risks. Lenders can benefit from pooled data and shared intelligence, highlighting trends and risks that might not be evident in isolated datasets. For example, collaborations among banks can lead to industry-wide early warning systems, flagging emerging risks that could affect multiple institutions.

Lastly, it's vital to align credit risk assessment with the broader goals of the financial institution or portfolio. Understanding the risk appetite and strategic objectives ensures that the credit decisions support long-term sustainability rather than short-term gains. This alignment fosters a more resilient financial ecosystem, capable of withstanding economic volatility and sector-specific downturns.

Identifying credit risk is an evolving process requiring a blend of traditional methodologies, advanced technologies, human judgment, and regulatory compliance. By leveraging these facets, financial professionals can make informed decisions that safeguard investments, enhance portfolio performance, and contribute to overall economic stability.

Managing and Mitigating Counterparty Risk

Managing and Mitigating Counterparty Risk is one of the most critical aspects to focus on when dealing with credit risk in financial markets. It involves identifying, evaluating, and addressing the financial health of parties you're engaging with so that you don't end up with significant losses down the line. Counterparty risk, essentially, is the risk that the other party in a transaction may not fulfill their end of the deal. This could stem from insolvency, liquidity issues, or other financial difficulties.

First and foremost, to effectively manage and mitigate counterparty risk, it's imperative to conduct thorough due diligence. This means assessing the creditworthiness of the counterparty before entering into any financial agreement. Credit ratings provided by agencies like Moody's, Standard & Poor's, and Fitch can be useful, but they shouldn't be your only source of information. Talk to industry contacts, review financial statements, and scrutinize any other available financial data. The more information you have, the better you'll be able to gauge the risk level.

One useful practice is to establish a comprehensive counterparty risk framework. This framework should include risk limits that are tailored to the financial health and creditworthiness of each counterparty. For instance, you might set lower exposure limits for parties with weaker credit scores and higher ones for those with robust financial metrics. These limits should be regularly reviewed and adjusted as needed, based on the evolving risk landscape and any new information.

Next, diversification is key. Don't put all your eggs in one basket by relying too heavily on a single counterparty. Spread your risk across multiple counterparties to minimize the impact if one defaults. In the realm of financial markets, the concept of diversification can't be overemphasized. By spreading your exposure, you ensure that a default by one counterparty will not be catastrophic to your overall portfolio.

In addition to diversification, collateral is another crucial tool for managing counterparty risk. By requiring counterparties to post collateral, you create a buffer that can protect you in the event they default. The type and amount of collateral should be proportional to the level of risk. It's also important to regularly mark-to-market the collateral to ensure it remains adequate over time.

Another strategy is to use netting arrangements, which allow you to offset obligations with the same counterparty. This can significantly reduce the principal amount at risk. Netting can be particularly useful in situations where multiple transactions are involved, as it simplifies the management of overall exposure.

Legal agreements are a critical line of defense. Ensure that all financial transactions are governed by robust legal agreements, such as International Swaps and Derivatives Association (ISDA) agreements. These agreements outline the terms and conditions, including provisions for collateral, netting, and default. Having a clear legal framework can help you efficiently deal with counterparty defaults, minimizing potential losses.

Technology and analytics play an increasingly important role in managing counterparty risk. Utilize sophisticated risk management software to analyze real-time data and assess counterparty risk dynamically. These tools can help in monitoring credit exposure, tracking collateral, and conducting stress tests to evaluate how various scenarios might impact counterparty risk.

For large institutions, setting up a dedicated counterparty risk management team can be beneficial. These teams focus solely on assessing and managing the risk of counterparties, ensuring that all transactions are continually evaluated for potential risk. Their expertise can provide valuable insights and allow for more agile responses to changes in the financial health of counterparties.

Regular stress testing and scenario analysis are also essential. These tools help you understand how your portfolio might perform under adverse conditions, such as financial crises, economic downturns, or disruptions in specific markets. By simulating these scenarios, you can identify vulnerabilities and take preemptive measures to shore up your defenses.

Lastly, stay informed and adaptable. Financial markets and economic conditions are ever-changing, and so is counterparty risk. Regularly update your risk models, review your exposure, and stay attuned to any shifts in the creditworthiness of your counterparties. An adaptable approach ensures that you're not caught off guard by sudden changes in the risk landscape.

In summary, **Managing and Mitigating Counterparty Risk** involves a multi-faceted approach that includes thorough due diligence, establishing risk frameworks, diversification, using collateral, legal agreements, leveraging technology, setting up dedicated teams, stress testing, and staying adaptable. By incorporating these practices, you can significantly reduce the potential impact of counterparty defaults and protect your financial interests effectively.

Chapter 9:
Operational Risk Management

Operational Risk Management delves into the intricacies of identifying, assessing, and mitigating risks that stem from day-to-day business operations. This chapter underscores the significance of establishing robust control mechanisms to ensure that unforeseen disruptions don't derail your financial goals. From system failures and human errors to fraud and cybersecurity threats, operational risks are ubiquitous and evolving. Hence, building a resilient framework with proactive assessment and meticulous recovery planning becomes critical. This chapter aims to equip you with the knowledge to create comprehensive strategies, addressing both the immediate and long-term challenges, thereby safeguarding your investment portfolio from internal vulnerabilities. The focus is not just on prevention but also on recovery, offering a balanced approach to effective operational risk management.

Assessing Operational Risk

Assessing Operational Risk starts with understanding that operational risk is the potential for loss resulting from inadequate or failed internal processes, people, systems, or external events. Unlike market or credit risk, which are more easily quantified, operational risk requires a thorough qualitative analysis. It encompasses everything from human errors and system failures to fraud and natural disasters. Because it is so multifaceted, assessing operational risk demands a comprehensive approach, blending both qualitative insights and quantitative tools.

One effective methodology for operational risk assessment is the risk and control self-assessment (RCSA). This process involves systematically identifying potential operational risks across various business units and functions. During an RCSA, departments evaluate their own processes, identifying vulnerable areas and assessing the effectiveness of existing controls. This self-assessment is typically backed by workshops, interviews, and detailed questionnaires. By engaging multiple layers of an organization, RCSA builds a culture of risk awareness and accountability.

Another important component of assessing operational risk is the use of key risk indicators (KRIs). KRIs are metrics that provide early warning signals of increasing risk exposures in specific areas. For example, a rise in the number of system outages or an increase in customer complaints can serve as indicators of underlying operational weaknesses. By monitoring these indicators, organizations can take proactive measures to mitigate risks before they materialize into significant losses.

Scenario analysis is also a crucial tool in operational risk assessment. By envisioning worst-case and best-case scenarios, organizations can gauge the potential impact of various risk events. This process not only helps in understanding the severity of risks but also in formulating relevant contingency plans. For instance, in a scenario where a natural disaster disrupts business operations, organizations can plan for backup facilities and data recovery processes to ensure continuity.

While qualitative methods provide valuable insights, quantitative approaches cannot be ignored when assessing operational risk. Techniques such as loss distribution approach (LDA) involve analyzing historical loss data to model the frequency and severity of operational risk events. By leveraging statistical tools, organizations can estimate potential losses and allocate capital reserves accordingly. This data-driven approach not only enhances precision in risk assessment but also helps in regulatory compliance.

Human factors are a significant source of operational risk, and assessing this aspect requires a nuanced understanding of organizational culture and behavior. Employee training and awareness programs play a crucial role in mitigating human-related risks. Regular training ensures that staff are well-versed in risk management protocols and are adept at identifying and reporting potential risks. A culture that encourages open communication and ethical behavior is fundamental in controlling human factors that contribute to operational risk.

Technology-related risks are another critical facet of operational risk assessment. In today's digital age, cybersecurity threats are ever-present, and the consequences of a breach can be severe. Regular audits of IT systems and networks are essential to identify vulnerabilities. Moreover, investing in robust cybersecurity measures, such as encryption and multi-factor authentication, can significantly reduce exposure to technology-related risks. Continuous monitoring and updating of IT infrastructure are vital to staying ahead of emerging threats.

External risks, often beyond an organization's control, also need to be considered when assessing operational risk. These can range from geopolitical events to natural disasters. While these risks are unpredictable, having a well-defined crisis management plan can mitigate their impact. The plan should include detailed protocols for emergency response, communication strategies, and resource allocation. Collaborating with external stakeholders, such as government agencies and non-profits, can also enhance an organization's resilience to external shocks.

The role of leadership in assessing and managing operational risk cannot be overstated. Senior management must demonstrate a commitment to robust risk management practices. This involves setting the tone at the top, promoting a risk-aware culture, and ensuring that adequate resources are allocated for risk management activities. Additionally, leadership should periodically review risk management policies and practices to ensure they remain effective and relevant in a constantly evolving risk landscape.

Integrating operational risk assessment into the broader enterprise risk management (ERM) framework is essential for a holistic risk management strategy. ERM provides a structured approach to identify, assess, and manage risks across the entire organization. By viewing operational risk within the context of other risk categories, such as market and credit risk, organizations can better understand interdependencies and potential compound effects. This integrated perspective supports more informed decision-making and resource allocation.

Regulatory expectations also play a significant role in shaping operational risk assessment practices. Regulatory bodies, such as the Basel Committee on Banking Supervision, have established guidelines and standards for operational risk management. Compliance with these regulations is not only a legal requirement but also serves as a benchmark for best practices. Regularly reviewing and updating risk management frameworks to align with regulatory standards ensures that organizations remain compliant and mitigate potential legal and financial penalties.

Finally, continuous improvement is a cornerstone of effective operational risk assessment. Organizations must remain vigilant and adaptable, learning from past incidents and near-misses. Establishing a feedback loop, where lessons learned are incorporated into risk management practices, fosters an environment of continuous improvement. Regularly revisiting and refining risk assessment processes ensures that they evolve in line with new risks and changing circumstances, thereby enhancing an organization's resilience.

In summary, **Assessing Operational Risk** requires a multi-dimensional approach that integrates both qualitative and quantitative methods. It involves self-assessments, key risk indicators, scenario analysis, and a strong focus on human and technology-related factors. Leadership, regulatory compliance, and continuous improvement are essential elements in this comprehensive strategy. By effectively assessing operational risk, organizations can safeguard themselves against potential losses, ensure smoother operations, and create a resilient foundation for sustainable growth.

Control Mechanisms and Recovery Planning

These form the backbone of any robust operational risk management strategy. Effective control mechanisms are vital in preventing potential risks from escalating into disruptive financial losses. They help ensure that a company's operations remain aligned with its risk tolerance, facilitating smooth business processes and safeguarding stakeholder interests.

First, let's delve into the various control mechanisms that corporations can employ. Internal controls are perhaps the most fundamental. These are processes and procedures implemented within a company to ensure the integrity of financial and accounting information, promote accountability, and prevent fraud. Having a strong internal control system means implementing policies like segregation of duties, physical controls (such as access restrictions), and regular internal audits. This level of scrutiny and oversight helps catch irregularities before they can become significant issues.

Risk identification is the first and perhaps most critical step in this process. Companies should employ comprehensive risk assessment methodologies to identify and measure potential operational risks.

This involves continuous monitoring of various risk indicators, both financial and non-financial. Financial professionals will appreciate that a deep understanding of market dynamics, regulatory requirements, and internal vulnerabilities is essential for effective risk identification and subsequent control.

Quantitative risk assessment tools, such as Value at Risk (VaR) and stress testing, play crucial roles here. VaR, for example, provides a probabilistic estimate of the maximum potential loss in a portfolio over a given time frame, under normal market conditions. Stress testing, on the other hand, evaluates how extreme market scenarios would impact the portfolio. These tools help in proactively identifying vulnerabilities and forming control strategies accordingly.

Moving from identification to response, the development of an effective risk response strategy is key. Think of this as proactively planning how to handle risks as they materialize. This encompasses not just mitigation, but also acceptance, transfer, and avoidance strategies. For instance, establishing an emergency fund or using insurance policies can act as financial buffers against specific types of risks.

In terms of operational control mechanisms, technology plays a pivotal role. Automation can significantly enhance risk management processes. Implementing advanced analytics, artificial intelligence, and machine learning algorithms can offer predictive insights, identifying potential risk events before they occur. Technologies like blockchain ensure data integrity and transparency, making it more challenging for fraudulent activities to go undetected. On the flip side, reliance on technology also introduces cyber risks, which must be countered with robust IT governance and cybersecurity measures.

A well-designed risk reporting framework is another critical control mechanism. Transparent and timely reporting ensures that stakeholders are kept informed about the current risk landscape and effectiveness of controls. Regular risk assessment reports, audit findings, and compliance checks must be communicated to senior management and, where applicable, to regulators. This kind of open communication fosters an environment of accountability and continuous improvement.

Effective governance frameworks, comprising clear roles and responsibilities, robust policies, and consistent oversight, underpin all other control mechanisms. The board of directors, senior management, and risk committees play critical roles in this regard. They must ensure that risk management approaches align with the company's strategic objectives and regulatory requirements.

Now, let's address recovery planning, a crucial aspect that guarantees business continuity in the event of a crisis. At its core, recovery planning involves developing and implementing strategies to quickly restore normal operations after a disruption. This includes creating a comprehensive Business Continuity Plan (BCP) and Disaster Recovery Plan (DRP).

A Business Continuity Plan outlines procedures and instructions an organization must follow in the face of disaster – whether it's a cyber-attack, a natural disaster, or other crisis. The BCP encompasses guidelines on maintaining essential functions during and after a disaster and puts in place strategies for data and operational recovery. Key components include business impact analysis, risk assessment, and recovery strategies, along with ongoing testing and updating of the plan to ensure its effectiveness.

Disaster Recovery Plans, meanwhile, zero in on the IT and data components of the continuity strategy. A DRP features specific policies for dealing with technological disruptions, including data recovery procedures, alternate communication paths, and backup sites. It's essential that the DRP is tested and validated through regular drills, ensuring that all team members are familiar with their roles during an actual event.

An important facet of recovery planning is the human element. Not only should the plans address technological and operational recovery, but they must also consider the well-being and safety of employees. Ensuring that personnel are trained and understand their responsibilities during a crisis is paramount. Regular training sessions and mock drills can significantly bolster preparedness.

Furthermore, the financial aspect cannot be ignored. Maintaining financial resiliency through sufficient liquidity and access to credit lines is critical. Businesses should have a financial contingency plan that details steps to stabilize finances, secure additional funding if necessary, and allocate emergency funds efficiently. This financial foresight ensures that businesses can weather the immediate impact of crises and sustain long-term recovery.

Integration is the final piece of the puzzle. It's essential that control mechanisms and recovery plans are integrated into the overall strategic framework of the organization. They shouldn't exist as isolated components but as dynamic parts of a cohesive risk management strategy. This integration ensures that respond and recovery activities are harmonious and swift, minimizing downtime and preserving stakeholder confidence.

In conclusion, **Control Mechanisms and Recovery Planning** are instrumental in a company's overarching risk management approach. From proactive risk identification and the establishment of internal controls to the creation of robust recovery plans, these strategies collectively reinforce an organization's resilience. For investors, financial planners, and risk managers, these mechanisms provide the security and confidence necessary to navigate the complex landscape of financial risk. They are the unsung heroes ensuring that business operations remain uninterrupted and financial assets protected, irrespective of the challenges that may surface.

Chapter 10:
Legal and Regulatory Compliance

In the complex world of finance, legal and regulatory compliance isn't just a necessity—it's a cornerstone of sustainable investing. By diligently navigating evolving financial regulations and adhering to legal standards, investors and financial professionals can safeguard their portfolios against unforeseen legal risks and penalties. Whether it's understanding the nuances of SEC regulations, adhering to international compliance standards, or implementing robust internal controls, staying compliant helps protect both assets and reputation. It's not just about avoiding fines; effective compliance practices foster trust with clients and stakeholders, providing a robust foundation for long-term success. As we explore the landscape of legal and regulatory requirements in this chapter, remember that vigilance in compliance isn't merely a regulatory box to check—it's an integral part of strategic risk management that enhances overall investment resilience.

Navigating Financial Regulations

The ability to navigate financial regulations requires a deep understanding of the ever-evolving legal landscape that governs financial markets. In the world of investing and finance, regulatory frameworks are in place to ensure transparency, protect investors, and maintain stability. As complex as these regulations may seem, mastering them is absolutely essential for financial professionals. Investors and managers alike must be agile and knowledgeable to not only comply with these laws but also leverage them to safeguard their portfolios.

Governmental agencies like the Securities and Exchange Commission (SEC) in the United States, the Financial Conduct Authority (FCA) in the United Kingdom, and other international regulatory bodies set rules to ensure market integrity and protect against systemic risks. These bodies scrutinize everything from insider trading to the fiduciary obligations of fund managers. Understanding these guidelines can help you navigate the investment landscape and avoid legal pitfalls that could have severe financial repercussions.

One fundamental aspect of financial regulation is compliance. Companies and financial professionals must perform specific activities to comply with regulatory requirements. These obligations can range from conducting regular audits to submitting detailed reports that disclose financial conditions and risks. Compliance departments in financial firms take on this hefty responsibility, but knowledge of these regulations benefits everyone involved in financial transactions—from traders to asset managers.

Risk management is intrinsically tied to regulatory compliance. Regulatory bodies often update guidelines and introduce new policies in response to emerging risks. Staying informed about these changes is critical. For instance, the introduction of the Dodd-Frank Act after the 2008 financial crisis reshaped the landscape of risk management in the United States. This law brought significant changes, including stricter capital requirements and enhanced scrutiny of derivative markets. Ignorance of such regulations can lead to devastating penalties and even business shutdowns.

Understanding regulatory frameworks also empowers you to implement more effective risk management strategies. Legal requirements often mandate specific risk mitigation practices, such as diversification limitations and stress testing. For instance, regulations might require that mutual funds not have more than a certain percentage of their assets concentrated in a single investment. Adhering to these guidelines helps to spread risk and protect investors from severe losses.

Moreover, international financial regulations can add another layer of complexity. Various countries have specific regulations pertaining to foreign investments, fund transfers, and taxation. If you're managing a portfolio with international assets, being aware of different regulatory environments is crucial. The Foreign Account Tax Compliance Act (FATCA) in the U.S., for instance, affects how foreign financial institutions deal with American customers, imposing rigorous reporting requirements. Failure to comply can result in hefty fines and restrictions.

In addition to federal and international regulations, each state or province may have its own rules. For instance, certain U.S. states have additional guidelines for investment advisors and brokers. It's crucial to be aware of these requirements to maintain compliance on all fronts. Regularly consulting legal experts specializing in financial law can provide invaluable guidance and keep you abreast of new regulatory developments.

Technological advancements, such as artificial intelligence and blockchain, are affecting regulatory landscapes. Regulators are now focusing on adjusting existing frameworks to incorporate and regulate these advancements. For example, cryptocurrency has created new challenges for financial regulators worldwide. Guidelines are continually being updated to cover Blockchain technology and Initial Coin Offerings (ICOs), which present unique risks and opportunities. Keeping informed about these changes is essential for mitigating risks associated with modern technologies.

It's also vital to understand the spirit behind these regulations. While some investors and companies may view regulatory requirements as cumbersome, these laws aim to create a fair and transparent investing environment. They protect against fraud, market manipulation, and systemic risks that can destabilize economies. From an organizational perspective, building a culture of compliance can be advantageous. Companies that prioritize regulatory adherence often enjoy enhanced reputations and greater investor trust.

The role of compliance officers and regulatory experts cannot be overstated in this context. These professionals are tasked with interpreting complex laws to ensure that business operations align with regulatory demands. Continuous education and training programs for all employees involved in financial operations can also be instrumental. They help instill the importance of adherence to laws and elevate the overall quality of risk management practices within the firm.

Moreover, interacting with regulators isn't solely about compliance but also about cooperation and dialogue. Before implementing new regulations, many regulatory bodies often seek feedback from the industry. Engaging in these consultations can allow firms to influence the final guidelines and better prepare for upcoming changes. Such proactive involvement helps firms stay ahead of the curve, contributing to more effective risk management strategies.

Transparency is another key aspect enforced by financial regulations. Companies must disclose material information that affects their financial situation and investment performance. Such disclosures help investors make informed decisions and foster trust in the financial system. Efforts to conceal information could lead to severe legal repercussions, asset freezes, and significant harm to a firm's reputation.

Implementing a robust compliance program that integrates technology can further enhance adherence to financial regulations. Software solutions for compliance management can automate monitoring and documentation processes. These tools can help track regulatory changes in real time, ensuring that all aspects of risk management are continually updated.

Finally, regulatory environments will continue to evolve, influenced by political, economic, and technological factors. Therefore, staying educated and resilient is essential for navigating this complexity. Future financial professionals must adopt a mindset of continuous learning and adaptability. Gaining certifications like the Certified Regulatory and Compliance Professional (CRCP) or even advanced degrees specializing in financial law could offer an edge in understanding and managing these intricate regulatory environments.

To conclude, effectively navigating financial regulations is not an optional skill but a required competency for anyone serious about successful risk management in the finance sector. Mastering these regulations not only ensures compliance but also fortifies the integrity of your investment strategies. So, stay informed, be proactive, and leverage regulatory knowledge as a pillar of robust risk management.

Risk Management and Legal Compliance

These are two intertwined components crucial for sustaining a viable investment strategy, particularly in an era where regulatory landscapes constantly evolve. The importance of compliance with legal frameworks cannot be understated—non-compliance can lead to severe penalties, legal actions, and, ultimately, the demise of even the most successful investment ventures. Possessing a robust risk management framework is equally integral, as it helps to identify, analyze, and mitigate potential risks before they manifest into issues that could threaten the financial health of a portfolio or organization.

At the core of *Risk Management and Legal Compliance* lies the alignment of a firm's investment activities with prevailing financial regulations. These regulations are designed not only to protect investors but also to uphold the integrity of financial markets.

Navigating this landscape requires a dynamic approach, given that laws and guidelines can vary significantly by jurisdiction and are subject to frequent updates. Ensuring compliance, therefore, involves extensive research, continuous monitoring, and often the expertise of legal professionals proficient in financial legislation.

The complexities of modern financial markets demand a multifaceted risk management approach that accounts for various regulatory requirements. This includes adhering to standards set by institutions like the Securities and Exchange Commission (SEC), the Financial Industry Regulatory Authority (FINRA), and international bodies such as the International Organization of Securities Commissions (IOSCO). These institutions set out guidelines to ensure transparency, fairness, and accountability in financial activities. Ignoring these parameters is not an option—a fact underscored by high-profile cases where institutions faced hefty fines and reputational damage for regulatory breaches.

One fundamental aspect of this dual focus is maintaining **transparency and documentation**. Proper documentation serves multiple purposes: it demonstrates compliance, aids in audits, and provides a clear trail in case of disputes or investigations. For instance, detailed records of client interactions, investment decisions, and risk assessments help establish good governance practices and assure regulatory bodies of the firm's adherence to legal standards. Transparency in reporting and disclosures is also a cornerstone in strengthening investor confidence and maintaining market stability.

Risk management and legal compliance also extend to the realm of cyber security. In today's digital age, financial firms are increasingly vulnerable to cyber threats, which poses a significant operational risk. Regulatory bodies have recognized this and have put forward guidelines aimed at protecting sensitive financial data and ensuring business continuity in the event of a cyber attack. As such, compliance now involves robust cyber security measures, regular audits, and a proactive stance on safeguarding information systems.

Financial institutions must engage in *regular training and development* for their staff to stay ahead of regulatory changes and optimize their risk management protocols. Knowledgeable and well-trained employees are an asset in fostering a culture of compliance and risk awareness. Training programs can cover topics such as the identification of emerging risks, updates on regulatory changes, ethical standards in financial transactions, and the use of technology in monitoring compliance. This continuous education helps in building expertise within the organization, ensuring that all personnel are aligned with both risk management and legal compliance objectives.

Coming to the vital role of **technology in compliance**, Regulatory Technology, or RegTech, has emerged as a game-changer. RegTech solutions leverage advanced technologies like Artificial Intelligence (AI), machine learning, and big data analytics to streamline the compliance process. These technologies can automate the monitoring of regulatory updates, compliance reporting, and risk assessment tasks, making them more efficient and less prone to human error. This not only reduces the administrative burden on compliance teams but also enhances the accuracy and reliability of compliance efforts.

There's also the aspect of *international compliance* that financial entities must consider, especially those with cross-border operations. Different countries have different compliance requirements, and a firm must harmonize its operations with the regulatory frameworks of each jurisdiction it operates in. For instance, aligning with the General Data Protection Regulation (GDPR) in the European Union while concurrently meeting the Financial Services and Markets Act requirements in the UK demands meticulous attention and versatile compliance programs.

Integrating ethical practices into risk management and legal compliance frameworks can significantly amplify their effectiveness. Ethical standards create a strong foundation where compliance isn't just about following laws but also about doing what's right. Encouraging ethical behavior within the organization reduces the likelihood of fraudulent activities and enhances the firm's reputation. Investors and clients are more likely to trust an institution known for its ethical operations, thereby fostering long-term relationships and sustainable growth.

Another critical element in this discussion is the role of **senior management and the board of directors**. Effective risk management and legal compliance must begin at the top. Leaders must set the tone for a culture that prioritizes these aspects, developing policies and procedures that reflect this commitment. Regular board meetings should include comprehensive reviews of compliance and risk management reports, ensuring accountability and encouraging transparency. The board should also ensure that adequate resources are allocated for compliance and risk management activities, recognizing that scrimping in these areas could lead to significant future liabilities.

In conclusion, the intersection of **Risk Management and Legal Compliance** represents a multifaceted challenge that demands constant vigilance, adaptability, and a proactive approach. By fostering a culture that values compliance and risk management, leveraging technology, ensuring robust documentation, and continuously educating staff, financial firms can mitigate risks and maintain regulatory adherence. This balanced approach not only safeguards the firm's reputation and assets but also contributes to the overall health and stability of financial markets. Investing in these practices is not just a legal obligation—it's a strategic imperative that underpins sustainable success in the competitive world of finance.

Chapter 11:
Advanced Risk
Management Techniques

Tackling sophisticated and multifaceted risk scenarios requires a robust toolkit of advanced techniques that extend beyond traditional methods. Embarking on this journey, we'll delve into dynamic hedging and derivatives—powerful instruments that can shield portfolios from the ravages of unexpected market moves. Simultaneously, stress testing and Extreme Value Theory (EVT) offer a lens to scrutinize and fortify against rare, yet devastating, market upheavals. By mastering these advanced methodologies, investors and professionals can not only protect but potentially enhance the resilience and performance of their investments. The insight and application of these techniques cultivate a proactive, rather than reactive, stance in risk management, empowering you to foresee and navigate the complex financial landscapes with confidence.

Dynamic Hedging and Derivatives

These are powerful tools in the hands of a savvy investor or risk manager. In today's financial landscape, where market conditions can change in the blink of an eye, dynamic hedging provides flexibility and precision in managing risk. At its core, dynamic hedging involves adjusting hedge positions as market conditions change, effectively allowing for real-time risk management. This is particularly valuable for portfolios containing assets with high levels of volatility or those that are exposed to significant market fluctuations.

Let's begin by understanding what "dynamic hedging" truly entails. Unlike traditional static hedging, which maintains a fixed hedge ratio over time, dynamic hedging is about adaptability. Imagine you're steering a ship through rough waters. Static hedging would be like setting your sail and hoping the winds remain constant. Dynamic hedging, on the other hand, is akin to adjusting your sail and rudder continuously to navigate changing conditions. This adaptability means that your investment portfolio is always protected against adverse movements, enabling you to lock in gains and mitigate losses effectively.

Derivatives are the instruments that make dynamic hedging possible. Futures, options, swaps, and other derivative contracts provide the necessary leverage and flexibility. These financial instruments derive their value from an underlying asset, such as stocks, bonds, commodities, or even interest rates. By using derivatives, you can hedge against price movements without having to own the underlying asset in large quantities. This allows for a more efficient allocation of capital and potentially higher returns on investment.

To illustrate, imagine managing a portfolio of tech stocks, which tend to be highly volatile. You might employ options contracts to hedge against potential downside risk. When the market outlook changes, you can adjust your hedge by buying or selling additional options contracts or changing the strike prices and expiration dates of existing ones. This tactical adjustment is the essence of dynamic hedging. By continuously recalibrating the hedge, you get a tailored solution that responds to market movements in real-time.

Why resort to dynamic hedging and derivatives, you ask? For one, the financial markets are more interconnected and complex than ever before. The traditional methods of risk management, which might involve simple diversification or static hedging, often prove inadequate. Dynamic hedging offers a proactive approach, allowing you to stay ahead of market trends rather than reacting to them after the fact. Moreover, derivatives provide opportunities for cost-effective hedging. They often require lower upfront costs compared to outright transactions of the underlying assets.

Consider the strategy known as delta hedging, a form of dynamic hedging used in options trading. Delta measures the sensitivity of an option's price to changes in the price of the underlying asset. By adjusting the hedge ratio according to delta, traders can neutralize the portfolio's exposure to small price movements. This involves buying or selling the underlying asset to offset the changes in delta. The beauty of delta hedging lies in its precision; it offers protection without the need to overhaul the entire portfolio.

Another pertinent strategy is the use of variance swaps, which allow investors to hedge against volatility itself rather than price movements. These swaps settle based on the realized variance (or volatility) of the underlying asset over a specific period. This can be particularly useful when market conditions are expected to become turbulent, and traditional hedges might not provide sufficient protection. By leveraging variance swaps, you can create a shield against market volatility, ensuring that your portfolio remains resilient.

However, it's crucial to recognize that dynamic hedging and derivatives are not a panacea. They come with their own set of challenges and risks. For one, the cost of constantly adjusting hedges can add up, potentially eating into your returns. Additionally, derivatives carry counterparty risk—the risk that the other party in the contract might default. To mitigate these risks, rigorous risk management processes and robust financial models are essential. Understanding the nuances of each derivative instrument and how it fits within your broader strategy is equally important.

Furthermore, dynamic hedging requires a deep understanding of the market and a keen sense of timing. It's not just about having the right tools but knowing when and how to use them. This often involves advanced quantitative methods and real-time data analytics. Techniques such as Monte Carlo simulations and scenario analysis can help predict potential market movements and inform hedge adjustments. Moreover, staying updated with market trends and geopolitical events can provide valuable insights into potential risks and opportunities.

A practical example is the use of interest rate swaps by corporations to manage exposure to fluctuating interest rates. Suppose a company has issued debt with a variable interest rate but prefers a fixed rate to predict future obligations accurately. By entering into an interest rate swap, the company can exchange the variable rate payments for fixed-rate payments, effectively locking in a stable interest expense. As market conditions change, the terms of the swap can be adjusted to maintain the desired exposure, demonstrating the dynamic aspect of the strategy.

In the world of dynamic hedging, technology plays a vital role. Advanced algorithms and high-frequency trading systems can execute hedge adjustments in milliseconds, far quicker than a human could. Machine learning models can analyze vast amounts of data to predict market movements and optimize hedging strategies. Using these technologies enables more precise and timely adjustments, enhancing the effectiveness of dynamic hedging.

Inspiring investors to embrace dynamic hedging and derivatives also involves highlighting their potential for transforming portfolios. When executed skillfully, these strategies can turn volatile markets into opportunities for profit, rather than mere threats. Drawing inspiration from seasoned traders and financial experts who successfully navigate these tools can provide the motivation and confidence needed to incorporate them into your own risk management practices.

With dynamic hedging and derivatives, you're not merely reacting to market movements; you're anticipating them and adapting proactively. This foresight and adaptability can differentiate between a portfolio that merely survives and one that thrives, even in the most challenging market conditions. By leveraging these advanced risk management techniques, you position yourself not just to mitigate risk, but to seize opportunities for growth and profit.

In conclusion, dynamic hedging and derivatives offer a sophisticated approach to managing investment risk. While they require a high degree of expertise and vigilance, the benefits they provide can be substantial. By integrating these strategies into your risk management toolkit, you equip yourself with the means to navigate the uncertainties of financial markets confidently and successfully.

Stress Testing and Extreme Value Theory

These two concepts are critical elements in modern risk management strategies, aiming to provide a robust assessment of how investment portfolios will respond under severe market conditions. Stress testing involves simulating extreme scenarios to understand how portfolios react to significant stressors. It goes beyond the usual day-to-day fluctuations by incorporating extraordinary events such as financial crises, economic recessions, or abrupt regulatory changes. Through this, investors can gauge the resilience of their portfolios and identify vulnerabilities that might not be evident under normal circumstances.

For a financial professional, stress testing is akin to conducting a fire drill. It's preparation for the unpredictable and a way to ensure that every part of the investment strategy is capable of withstanding 'worst-case' scenarios. The process begins by selecting a set of extreme yet plausible scenarios. These might include historical events like the

2008 financial crisis, geopolitical upheavals, or hypothetical situations such as a sudden spike in interest rates or an unforeseen natural disaster. The idea is to cover a spectrum of potential risks that could severely impact financial portfolios.

Imagine a portfolio manager overseeing a diverse set of assets. Through stress testing, she might discover that her portfolio is highly sensitive to interest rate changes. Armed with this knowledge, she can take preemptive actions such as adjusting her asset allocation or employing hedging strategies to mitigate potential losses. Hence, stress testing serves as both a diagnostic and a prescriptive tool, offering insights that guide strategic adjustments.

The next integral component is Extreme Value Theory (EVT). EVT addresses the tail ends of the distribution of returns, focusing on the rare but impactful events that can lead to substantial financial losses. Traditional statistical methods often underestimate the probability and impact of these extreme events because they rely on normal distribution assumptions, which don't account for the 'fat tails' observed in real financial markets.

EVT provides a framework to model and quantify the risks associated with these extreme events. By analyzing the maximum or minimum values in a data series, EVT helps predict the likelihood of catastrophic losses. For example, in insurance, EVT is used to estimate the probability of rare natural disasters, enabling better preparation and financial resilience.

Integrating EVT into stress testing enhances the robustness of risk management strategies. While stress testing explores the outcomes of predefined scenarios, EVT allows for the quantification of risks that fall outside the scope of these scenarios. Together, they provide a comprehensive view of both predictable and unpredictable risks, enabling a more nuanced and informed approach to investment risk management.

Let's consider a practical application. A portfolio manager may use stress testing to simulate a scenario where stock markets crash by 30%. She'd analyze the portfolio's performance under such a downturn, identifying which assets are most vulnerable and which might offer some protective diversification. Using EVT, she can further quantify the probability of such a crash, providing a statistical grounding to her stress test. This combination of forecast modeling and empirical analysis ensures that she's not only prepared for potential downturns but also has a clear understanding of their likelihood and impact.

The insights garnered from stress testing and EVT are invaluable for crafting risk mitigation strategies. Stress testing results might prompt portfolio rebalancing, increased cash reserves, or strategic allocation to more resilient asset classes like bonds or commodities. Meanwhile, EVT can inform the design of insurance products, derivatives, and other risk transfer mechanisms that protect against tail risks.

Investors and financial planners will find these tools indispensable as they navigate the complexities of today's financial landscapes. Markets are inherently unpredictable, and while it's impossible to foresee every potential risk, stress testing and EVT provide a solid foundation for preparedness. They aren't just about surviving the worst-case scenarios but thriving amidst uncertainty by preemptively addressing vulnerabilities.

It's important to realize that stress testing and EVT are dynamic processes. As markets evolve, new risks emerge, necessitating continuous updating and refinement of stress test scenarios and EVT models. For instance, the rise of cyber threats and geopolitical tensions are relatively modern concerns that must be integrated into contemporary stress tests. EVT might, in turn, need recalibration to account for the changing statistical probabilities of these new risks.

Institutions increasingly rely on advanced computational techniques and big data analytics to enhance these methodologies. Machine learning algorithms can identify patterns and correlations in vast datasets, providing deeper insights into potential risks and helping to refine stress testing scenarios. Similarly, big data can offer more accurate extreme value modeling by incorporating a broader array of predictors and historical data points.

The collaborative nature of risk management also comes into play here. Sharing insights from stress testing and EVT across departments and with stakeholders ensures a comprehensive organizational preparedness. Financial professionals across roles—from fund managers to compliance officers—benefit from a unified approach to risk management, facilitating better coordination and quicker response to potential crises.

Case studies further illuminate the practical benefits. For instance, during the COVID-19 pandemic, companies with rigorous stress testing frameworks could quickly pivot and adjust their strategies, mitigating losses and capitalizing on emerging opportunities. EVT models would have helped these firms gauge the likelihood and potential impact of such a global event, ensuring they weren't caught entirely off-guard.

In summary, **Stress Testing and Extreme Value Theory** are indispensable in the toolbox of any astute financial professional. They provide the dual benefit of diagnosing potential weaknesses and prescribing actionable strategies to fortify portfolios against extreme market conditions. In an environment where financial stability is increasingly under threat from a range of unpredictable sources, leveraging these advanced risk management techniques is not just advisable—it's essential. Investing in robust stress testing and EVT frameworks ensures that you're not just reacting to market changes but proactively preparing for them, safeguarding your financial future and enhancing your investment performance.

Chapter 12:
Risk Management in Practice

In the real world, the principles and theories of risk management come to life through a structured yet adaptive approach, as demonstrated in various case studies that highlight both successful strategies and notable failures. For investors and financial professionals, embedding these risk management techniques into daily operations isn't just beneficial; it's essential for long-term stability and growth. By constantly reassessing and adjusting risk strategies, businesses can deftly navigate market uncertainties and regulatory demands. This chapter delves into practical applications, focusing on how to seamlessly integrate risk management practices into business processes, ensuring they are part of the organizational culture and decision-making framework. Whether it's through the meticulous analysis of risk or the dynamic adjustments to portfolios, the end goal remains the same: protecting investments while cultivating growth opportunities. As we explore these facets, remember the true value of risk management lies in its ability to transform potential threats into strategic advantages.

Case Studies: Successes and Failures

Case studies offer a crucial lens into the tangible impact of risk management strategies. By examining real-world examples, we can extract valuable insights and better understand the nuances that define success or lead to failure. This lays the groundwork for crafting more resilient investment portfolios and devising advanced risk mitigation techniques.

One notable success story is the case of Goldman Sachs during the 2007-2008 financial crisis. While many financial institutions found themselves on the brink of collapse, Goldman Sachs navigated the turmoil with relative ease. By strategically shorting the subprime mortgage market, they not only hedged their risks but also turned a significant profit. This instance underscores the importance of proactive risk management and the value of executing well-timed, contrarian strategies. Their meticulous attention to risk indicators and dynamic hedging mechanisms provided a layer of defense that many of their contemporaries lacked.

On the flip side, we have the infamous failure of Long-Term Capital Management (LTCM) in the late 1990s. Despite being managed by Nobel laureates and leveraging sophisticated mathematical models, LTCM faced catastrophic losses. The fundamental mistake lay in their overreliance on quantitative models, which failed to account for extreme market conditions. Additionally, their excessive leverage magnified the impact of their losses exponentially. LTCM's downfall serves as a cautionary tale about the dangers of overconfidence in models and the risks associated with high leverage.

Another compelling success comes from the domain of asset management, specifically Ray Dalio's Bridgewater Associates. Bridgewater's "Pure Alpha" strategy has been a tremendous success, focusing heavily on diversification to manage risk. The firm employs a unique "risk parity" approach, balancing risk rather than capital. By doing so, Bridgewater has managed to achieve consistent returns across various market conditions, underscoring the power of well-executed diversification and strategic asset allocation.

In contrast, consider the failure of Archegos Capital Management in 2021. Archegos employed high leverage through total return swaps, accumulating significant positions in a few stocks. When the value of these stocks plummeted, margin calls were triggered, leading to a forced liquidation of positions. The firm's collapse highlights the dangers of concentrated positions and unregulated financial instruments. It emphasizes the need for rigorous stress testing and diversified portfolios to hedge against significant market downturns.

Incorporating risk management into corporate finance, we can examine General Electric's (GE) strategic errors in the early 2000s. GE's aggressive expansion into financial services exposed the company to a myriad of financial risks. When the 2008 crisis hit, GE Capital's troubles caught up, causing a liquidity crunch. Their inability to foresee the compounded risks of over-expansion and market volatility underscores the importance of aligning risk management practices with corporate strategy.

On the contrary, Aflac, the insurer, provides a shining example of effective risk management. During the 2008 financial crisis, Aflac maintained rigorous investment guidelines that emphasized liquidity and diversification, which helped them avoid the pitfalls that plagued other firms. Their commitment to a conservative investment philosophy paid off, allowing them to weather the crisis and emerge more robust. This case underscores the importance of disciplined investment policies and maintaining adequate liquidity reserves.

Looking at hedging strategies, Delta Airlines offers an instructive example. Delta locks in fuel prices using commodity futures and options, protecting against the volatility of jet fuel costs. This hedging strategy has shielded the company from the unpredictable swings in fuel prices, helping stabilize costs and plan more effectively. It's a practical application of using derivative instruments to manage operational risks, demonstrating the effectiveness of hedging as a risk mitigation tool.

In the realm of technology, Apple's approach to supply chain risk management is noteworthy. Apple diversifies its suppliers and maintains stringent quality controls to mitigate risks associated with supply chain disruptions. They also engage in forward contracts for essential materials, ensuring price stability and supply continuity. This strategy has been crucial in maintaining their competitive edge and operational efficiency, offering a template for managing operational and supply chain risks effectively.

Conversely, the tech sector has also seen its share of failures, such as Nokia. Once a leader in mobile technology, Nokia failed to adapt to market changes and consumer preferences quickly. Their reluctance to embrace smartphone technology in a timely manner resulted in a significant loss of market share. The oversight demonstrates the peril of underestimating market risks and the importance of innovation in staying competitive. Nokia's lapse in strategic risk management resulted in a stark decline from its industry-leading position.

The pharmaceutical industry also offers valuable lessons. Johnson & Johnson's handling of the Tylenol crisis in the 1980s is often cited as a classic example of effective risk management. Faced with product tampering, the company swiftly recalled the product and introduced tamper-proof packaging, regaining consumer trust. Their proactive approach and commitment to transparency mitigated the risk to their brand and set new safety standards for the industry.

However, the Vioxx scandal by Merck tells a different story. Despite early warning signs that the drug posed cardiovascular risks, the company continued its aggressive marketing. Eventually, Vioxx was withdrawn from the market, leading to significant financial losses and damage to the company's reputation. This case highlights the catastrophic impact of ignoring or underestimating risks and underscores the importance of ethical considerations in risk management.

Another successful example involves Toyota's response to the 2011 earthquake and tsunami in Japan. The disaster severely disrupted global supply chains, but Toyota's robust risk management practices, including geographical diversification and early investment in Business Continuity Planning (BCP), allowed for a quicker recovery. They re-established production faster than many competitors, minimizing financial impact and reinforcing their market position. This underscores the importance of preparing for rare but high-impact events through comprehensive risk management strategies.

In summary, these case studies provide a broad spectrum of learning opportunities. Whether it's Goldman Sachs' proactive hedging, LTCM's overreliance on quantitative models, or Aflac's conservative investment strategy, each offers unique insights. Successful risk management often combines accurate risk assessment, proactive strategy implementation, and a keen understanding of market and operational dynamics. As investors, financial planners, and corporate finance professionals, these lessons act as guiding stars, helping shape resilient and robust portfolios that can withstand the myriad uncertainties of the financial landscape.

Learning from both successes and failures can empower practitioners to be better prepared for future challenges. The critical takeaway is that a well-rounded approach to risk management, which includes both qualitative and quantitative techniques, strategic thinking, and ethical considerations, can significantly enhance an organization's ability to navigate the volatile terrain of financial markets. These case studies not only illustrate the pivotal role of risk management but also highlight the importance of continuous learning and adaptation in an ever-evolving financial world.

Integrating Risk Management into Business Operations

This requires more than just understanding theoretical principles or performing quantitative analysis—it's about weaving risk management into the very fabric of your organization's daily activities and strategic initiatives. Whether you're a financial planner, portfolio manager, or business owner, the key to a resilient and prosperous enterprise lies in establishing a thorough risk management culture. But how do we go about making risk management a seamless part of business operations?

First, it's imperative to recognize that for risk management to be effective, it should be a centralized aspect of the organization's overall strategy. This means aligning your company's risk appetite with its strategic objectives. One cannot overstate the importance of the collaboration between executive leadership and risk management teams in this alignment. Decisions made at the top affect the entire organization and set the tone for how risk is perceived and handled. Leadership should regularly communicate the significance of risk management, ensuring that it's understood and prioritized throughout the team.

Effective risk management integration also demands that risk identification be a continual process. Your organization should not only focus on well-known risks but also strive to unearth hidden threats that could jeopardize operations. Use a blend of quantitative tools, such as statistical models and scenario analyses, in conjunction with qualitative assessments like employee surveys and market research. The goal here is to construct a comprehensive risk profile that evolves as the organization grows and adapts to new challenges.

Embedding risk management into daily operations also necessitates robust training and education programs. Every employee, regardless of their role, should understand basic risk concepts and how their actions contribute to the organization's risk profile. Regular workshops and training sessions can keep the workforce informed about new risks and emerging best practices in risk management. Engaging employees in this manner fosters a proactive risk-aware culture, rather than one that simply reacts to problems as they arise.

Stakeholder engagement extends beyond employees. Shareholders, customers, suppliers, and even regulatory bodies can provide valuable insights into potential risks. Regular communication with these groups enhances transparency and trust, which can be vital when navigating crises. Moreover, considering stakeholders' insights when developing risk management strategies ensures a more holistic approach, addressing risks from multiple viewpoints.

An essential aspect of integrating risk management into business operations is the establishment of a risk management framework. This framework should outline policies, processes, and procedures for identifying, analyzing, and mitigating risks. It should also designate roles and responsibilities, so there's no ambiguity about who's accountable for what. Utilizing enterprise risk management (ERM) frameworks like COSO or ISO 31000 can provide structured approaches that accommodate the complexity of today's business environment.

Technology also plays a pivotal role in modern risk management. Implementing advanced software tools for risk monitoring, reporting, and analysis can drastically improve your organization's ability to manage risk effectively. These tools can provide real-time data and predictive analytics, enabling quicker and more informed decision-making. They also facilitate better communication between departments, ensuring that risk information is accurately and promptly disseminated.

Mainstreaming risk management also involves scenario planning and stress testing. These activities can help you anticipate and prepare for unlikely, but potentially devastating events. By simulating various adverse conditions, your organization can identify vulnerabilities and strengthen its defenses. This proactive stance not only mitigates potential impacts but also builds investor and client confidence in your resilience.

Another critical factor in integrating risk management into business operations is continuous improvement. Organizations should regularly review and update their risk management practices to ensure they're aligned with the current business environment and the company's objectives. This could involve periodic audits, feedback loops, and key performance metrics to measure the effectiveness of current strategies. Continuous improvement ensures that risk management remains dynamic and responsive to change.

Furthermore, effective risk communication is essential. Decision-makers need timely, accurate data to act on. Risk reports should be clear, concise, and actionable, offering insights into both the current risk landscape and future trends. Risk dashboards can offer a visual representation of risk metrics, making it easier for managers to grasp complex information quickly. Decision-makers armed with such tools can steer the organization with greater confidence.

It's also important to incorporate risk management objectives into performance evaluations and incentives. Employees are more likely to take risk management seriously if their contributions to risk mitigation are recognized and rewarded. Aligning incentives with risk management goals can lead to more diligent and innovative approaches to managing risks at all levels of the organization.

Finally, resilience must be a cornerstone of your risk management strategy. This means having robust contingency plans in place and ensuring that your organization can adapt to disruptions without significant loss. Business continuity planning, disaster recovery, and crisis management are all integral elements that support resilience. These plans should be tested regularly to ensure their effectiveness and updated as necessary to accommodate new risks.

Integrating risk management into business operations is not a one-time effort but an ongoing commitment. By embedding risk management deeply into your organizational culture, aligning it with strategic objectives, and utilizing advanced tools and frameworks, you can transform risk management from a reactive necessity into a proactive strength. This integration will not only protect your organization from potential pitfalls but also pave the way for sustained growth and profitability in an increasingly uncertain world. By viewing risk as a manageable part of your business operations, you set the stage for a more confident and robust future.

Online Review Request for This Book

If this book has enriched your understanding of risk management and provided valuable insights that you can apply in your professional endeavors, please take a moment to share your thoughts through an online review—your feedback helps others in the financial community discover and benefit from this resource.

Conclusion

We've explored the multifaceted world of risk management, diving deep into the theories, tools, and strategies that can safeguard and grow your investments. Risk is an inherent part of any financial journey, and understanding it is crucial to making informed decisions. From defining investment risks to advanced techniques in dynamic hedging and derivatives, this book has aimed to equip you with a comprehensive toolkit for navigating the complex landscape of financial risk.

One of the key takeaways is that risk management is not a one-size-fits-all solution. It requires a tailored approach, individual to each investor or portfolio. Your unique risk tolerance, investment goals, and market conditions will all play a role in shaping your risk management strategies. The importance of customizing your approach can't be overstated, and it's a theme that resonates through various chapters of this book.

Importance of diversification can't be understated either. While it's often cited as a basic principle, its role in mitigating risk holds profound implications for any portfolio. Diversification isn't just about spreading investments across various asset classes; it's about understanding the correlations between those assets and strategically positioning them to offset potential losses.

Quantitative and qualitative methods both serve as pillars of a robust risk management framework. Statistical tools, modeling techniques, and scenario analysis provide measurable insights. But qualitative considerations add critical context, factoring in human behavior, biases, and market sentiment. Combining these approaches allows for a more balanced, well-rounded understanding of risks.

Effective risk management also hinges on real-time adaptability. Markets are dynamic, and so should be your risk management strategies. Staying static in a fluid environment means exposing yourself to unforeseen vulnerabilities. Hence, the advanced techniques discussed, like dynamic hedging and stress testing, play an essential role in enabling this adaptability.

A crucial aspect we've discussed is the alignment of risk management with business operations and governance. This alignment isn't merely an operational necessity but a strategic imperative. Risk management should be embedded into the DNA of your organization, influencing decision-making processes at all levels. Educating and involving all stakeholders ensures a culture of risk awareness and proactive management.

Regulatory compliance is not just about abiding by laws; it's about understanding the broader implications of these regulations on your risk profile. Ensuring compliance while strategically managing risks positions you to take advantage of opportunities that align with regulatory frameworks.

Practical application often sheds light on the theoretical constructs we've studied. The case studies presented in this book illustrate how various organizations have successfully (or unsuccessfully) navigated risk landscapes. Learning from these real-world scenarios can provide invaluable insights and spur inspiration for your risk management practices.

As you move forward, remember that risk management is an ongoing process. It's not a checklist item that, once ticked off, is complete. Constant vigilance, regular reassessments, and updates to your risk management framework are essential. The financial world is continuously evolving, and staying ahead requires persistent effort.

To the investors, planners, analysts, and financial professionals reading this, the principles and practices detailed in this book are your allies. They offer pathways to mitigate losses and optimize returns, enabling you to make strategic, informed decisions. Embrace them, adapt them to your unique needs, and let them guide you toward safer, more prosperous financial ventures.

In conclusion, the knowledge gained from this book is both a shield and a compass. It protects your investments while guiding you through the complexities of the financial market. May your future endeavors be marked by informed choices, mitigated risks, and, ultimately, substantial rewards.

Appendix A:
Appendix

In this appendix, we've compiled essential tools and supplementary information aimed at reinforcing the concepts covered throughout the book. This section serves as a practical reference guide, making it easier for you to apply risk management principles effectively in your financial decision-making processes.

Risk Management Checklist

Utilize this comprehensive checklist to ensure that you're covering all vital aspects of risk management. This tool is designed to be a quick reference that aligns with the best practices discussed in the book:

- Risk Identification:
    - Have all potential risks been identified?
    - Are risks categorized appropriately (e.g., market, credit, operational)?
- Risk Assessment:
    - Have you assessed the impact and likelihood of each identified risk?
    - Are risk metrics calculated and updated regularly?
- Risk Tolerance:
    - Have you identified the risk tolerance levels for all stakeholders?

- o Are investor profiles regularly updated and matched with corresponding risk tolerance?
- Diversification:
  - o Is your asset allocation model revisited periodically?
  - o Are diversification strategies actively managed?
- Quantitative Analysis:
  - o Are statistical tools being used effectively to monitor risks?
  - o Is scenario analysis included in your risk assessment processes?
- Qualitative Considerations:
  - o Are behavioral biases being identified and mitigated?
  - o Is qualitative data incorporated in risk assessments?
- Regulatory Compliance:
  - o Are all legal and regulatory requirements met?
  - o Is compliance documentation kept up-to-date?
- Advanced Techniques:
  - o Are stress tests and dynamic hedges used appropriately?
  - o Is your extreme value theory modeling current and robust?

This checklist is a living document. Keep it handy and review it regularly to ensure that your risk management framework remains resilient and adaptable in the face of new challenges.

Additional Resources

While this book aims to cover all critical aspects of risk management, continuous learning and staying updated on new developments are essential. Consider exploring the following resources to deepen your knowledge:

- Financial industry journals and publications

- Professional associations such as GARP (Global Association of Risk Professionals) and PRMIA (Professional Risk Managers' International Association)

- Online courses and webinars from reputable financial education platforms

Conclusion

This appendix, and the checklist within, are designed to serve as a quick reference guide, aiding you in implementing effective risk management strategies. Remember, the goal is not just to understand risks but to manage and mitigate them proactively. Keep learning, stay vigilant, and apply these principles diligently to protect and grow your investments.

With these tools at your disposal, you're well-equipped to navigate the complex landscape of financial risk management. Best of luck in your journey towards more informed and confident financial decision-making.

Risk Management Checklist

This covers the pivotal action points ensuring a comprehensive and effective risk management strategy. While every investor and financial professional may approach risk management through a distinct lens, certain essential elements remain universal in crafting a resilient investment portfolio.

First on the checklist is the fundamental task of *identifying potential risks*. This involves a thorough analysis of both internal and external factors that could jeopardize investments. Internal factors might include company-specific issues such as management practices, financial health, and operational efficiencies, while external factors encompass market volatility, economic downturns, and geopolitical events. A comprehensive risk identification process ensures that no potential threat is left unexamined.

Once risks are identified, the next step is *risk assessment*. This entails evaluating the likelihood and potential impact of each identified risk. It's crucial to prioritize these risks based on their severity and probability. A high-probability, high-impact risk like a major market crash demands more immediate and robust mitigation strategies compared to low-probability, low-impact risks.

Moving forward, formulating *risk response strategies* is essential. There are several approaches to managing risk: avoidance, mitigation, transfer, and acceptance. Avoidance involves steering clear of high-risk investments. Mitigation means implementing measures to reduce the impact or likelihood of risk, while transfer includes techniques like insurance or hedging to shift the risk to another party. Finally, acceptance is a conscious decision to endure a risk, typically when the cost of mitigation exceeds the potential loss.

One indispensable element of an effective risk management checklist is *continuous monitoring and review*. The financial landscape is dynamic, and risk profiles can change rapidly. Regularly revisiting and updating the risk management plan ensures that new risks are promptly identified and managed. This continuous loop of assessment and adaptation keeps the strategy relevant and robust.

Clear communication and documentation are also paramount. It's important to document all risk management activities and decisions meticulously. This not only provides clarity and accountability but also serves as a valuable reference for future risk assessments. Additionally, maintaining open lines of communication with all stakeholders ensures that everyone is aware of the risks and the steps being taken to manage them.

Another critical aspect is *educating and training stakeholders*. Everyone involved in the investment process, from portfolio managers to analysts, should be well-versed in risk management principles and practices. This collective knowledge creates a cohesive approach to identifying, assessing, and managing risks, thereby enhancing the overall effectiveness of the risk management strategy.

Utilizing technology and analytical tools can significantly enhance risk management capabilities. Advanced analytical tools and financial software can provide valuable insights into risk factors and help in creating detailed predictive models. These technologies enable real-time risk monitoring and facilitate proactive rather than reactive risk management.

It's also beneficial to have a pre-determined *crisis management plan* in place. This plan should outline specific actions to be taken in the event of a significant risk event, such as a market crash or a sudden economic downturn. Having a clear, actionable plan ensures quick and effective response, thereby minimizing potential losses and stabilizing the investment portfolio.

Incorporating *stress testing and scenario analysis* into the risk management process is another crucial checklist item. These techniques allow investors to simulate various adverse conditions and evaluate the impact on their portfolios. By understanding how different scenarios would affect their investments, investors can better prepare and fortify their strategies against unforeseen events.

Effective *capital allocation and diversification* strategies are key components of risk management. Diversification spreads risk across different asset classes, sectors, and geographies, reducing the impact of any single investment's poor performance. Sound capital allocation ensures that resources are optimally distributed to balance risk and reward effectively.

Lastly, a robust risk management checklist should include *adherence to regulatory and compliance requirements.* Financial markets are governed by a myriad of regulations designed to protect investors and ensure market integrity. Staying compliant not only mitigates legal risks but also fosters trust and credibility with clients and stakeholders.

In conclusion, a thorough risk management checklist is indispensable for any investor or financial professional committed to safeguarding their investments. By diligently following these steps, one can create a resilient investment strategy capable of withstanding the uncertainties of the financial landscape. Remember, the essence of risk management lies not in avoiding risks altogether but in understanding and navigating them with confidence and foresight.

Glossary
of Risk Management Terms

This glossary aims to provide clear and concise definitions of essential terms and concepts in risk management. Understanding these terms will help you navigate the complexities of managing investment risks effectively.

Asset Allocation

The process of dividing investments among different asset categories like stocks, bonds, and cash to manage risk and achieve a desired risk-return profile.

Behavioral Biases

Psychological factors that can impact investors' decision-making, often leading to irrational financial decisions.

Credit Risk

The risk of loss arising from a borrower's failure to repay a loan or meet contractual obligations.

Counterparty Risk

The risk that the other party in a financial transaction will default or not meet contractual obligations.

Diversification

A risk management strategy that mixes a wide variety of investments within a portfolio to reduce exposure to any single asset or risk.

Dynamic Hedging

A strategy involving the frequent adjustment of hedging positions to protect a portfolio from risk due to fluctuating asset prices.

Extreme Value Theory (EVT)

A statistical approach to assess the risk of extreme events, commonly used in finance to evaluate the likelihood of rare but impactful market events.

Hedging

A risk management strategy used to offset potential losses in one investment by taking an opposite position in a related asset.

Key Risk Indicators (KRIs)

Metrics used to provide an early signal of increasing risk exposure in various areas of an organization.

Market Risk

The potential for losses due to factors that affect the overall performance of financial markets.

Operational Risk

The risk of loss resulting from inadequate or failed internal processes, people, systems, or external events.

Portfolio

A collection of financial investments like stocks, bonds, commodities, and cash equivalents held by an investor or an institution.

Quantitative Analysis

The use of mathematical and statistical methods to evaluate investment risks and opportunities.

Risk Management

The process of identification, assessment, and prioritization of risks followed by coordinated efforts to minimize, monitor, and control the probability or impact of unfortunate events.

Risk Tolerance

The degree of variability in investment returns that an individual or organization is willing to withstand.

Risk Response Strategies

Approaches to address identified risks, including risk avoidance, risk reduction, risk sharing, and risk retention.

Scenario Analysis

A process of analyzing possible future events by considering alternative possible outcomes (scenarios).

Stress Testing

A risk management technique that evaluates how financial assets or portfolios perform under adverse economic conditions.

Volatility

A statistical measure of the dispersion of returns for a given security or market index, often used to assess market risk.

Understanding these terms will equip you with the language and knowledge essential to navigate and implement effective risk management strategies. Armed with this foundation, you'll be better prepared to mitigate risks and safeguard your investments.

Key Risk Indicators and Metrics

These are crucial tools for anyone involved in the complex world of finance and investment. Understanding and actively monitoring these indicators can make the difference between navigating through turbulent times successfully or facing losses. Key Risk Indicators (KRIs) and Key Performance Indicators (KPIs) are often discussed together, but it's essential to understand that KRIs specifically focus on risk, providing early warnings of potential trouble ahead. These indicators serve as quantifiable measures used by organizations to gauge levels of risk in various domains.

For investors and financial professionals, KRIs are the linchpins of a robust risk management strategy. These metrics give insights into potential losses associated with various investment vehicles, guiding actions to mitigate such risks. When implemented effectively, KRIs enable a framework for proactive, rather than reactive, risk management, ensuring that one's portfolio remains resilient even in adverse conditions. The data captured can reflect both historical trends and potential future volatility, providing a comprehensive risk assessment.

Let's delve into what makes a KRI effective. Firstly, KRIs should be aligned with the overall risk appetite and threshold levels of the organization or individual investor. This alignment ensures that the indicators are meaningful and actionable. For example, for a portfolio manager, an effective KRI might measure the concentration risk of a particular asset class within the portfolio. By monitoring this metric, the portfolio manager can make informed decisions to diversify and limit exposure to high-risk investments.

Another essential aspect of KRIs is their specificity. Generic indicators yield limited actionable insights. Instead, focus on metrics that are specific and relevant to the unique risks faced by your investment portfolio. For instance, a corporate finance professional might track the interest rate risk by monitoring the duration and convexity of bonds held within the portfolio. Specific KRIs like these offer a more precise picture of risk and are easier to interpret and act upon.

Regular monitoring and updating of KRIs are vital for maintaining their effectiveness. Financial markets are inherently dynamic, and the risk landscape can change rapidly due to economic events, regulatory changes, or shifts in market sentiment. Hence, adopting a routine for reviewing and updating KRIs ensures that they remain relevant and provide timely warnings. This practice also includes back-testing different KRI thresholds against historical data to fine-tune them for better predictive power.

Now, you might wonder, what are some commonly used KRIs in the world of finance and investments? Volatility measures, such as the VIX index, serve as excellent indicators of market risk. They provide a snapshot of market expectations of volatility over a specific timeframe. This can be particularly useful for traders and investors in managing exposure to short-term market fluctuations. Credit ratings and credit default swap (CDS) spreads, on the other hand, are invaluable for assessing credit risk. They offer insights into the likelihood of default and the associated costs of insuring against such defaults.

In addition to these, liquidity metrics like bid-ask spreads or trading volumes give crucial information about the ease of entering or exiting positions in various assets. High bid-ask spreads or low trading volumes often indicate higher liquidity risk, signaling potential difficulties in realizing an asset's value quickly. For those involved in operational risk management, KRIs might include metrics like the frequency of system downtimes, the number of failed trades due to technological glitches, or compliance-related incidents.

Understanding the metrics themselves is one thing, but their interpretation and application are where the real value lies. Take VAR (Value at Risk), for example. VAR represents the maximum potential loss over a given time period at a specific confidence level. While it's a commonly used KRI, its limitations should be acknowledged. VAR assumes normal market conditions and may not account for extreme events or 'fat tails'. Therefore, supplementing VAR with other indicators like Conditional Value at Risk (CVaR) or stress testing results can provide a more rounded view of potential risks.

Incorporating various KRIs into a risk dashboard offers a comprehensive overview and facilitates quicker decision-making. A risk dashboard consolidates multiple indicators into a single, easily interpretable format, making it simpler for decision-makers to assess the risk environment. Such dashboards often use data visualization tools to highlight trends, anomalies, and areas that require immediate attention. This integration helps in not just identifying risk but also in devising and implementing mitigation strategies promptly.

Another critical aspect of KRIs is their regulatory significance. Many financial regulations mandate the monitoring and reporting of specific risk indicators. For example, Basel III guidelines require banks to maintain a detailed understanding of their liquidity and capital adequacy through specific metrics, like the Liquidity Coverage Ratio (LCR) and the Net Stable Funding Ratio (NSFR). Staying compliant with these requirements not only ensures regulatory adherence but also fortifies the organization's risk management practices.

The journey towards effective use of KRIs starts with choosing the right indicators. Begin by identifying key risk areas pertinent to your investment strategy or organizational focus. From there, select metrics that are both measurable and meaningful. Historical data analysis plays a critical role in this step, providing a basis for benchmarking and setting thresholds. Continuous improvement and adaptability in the choice and refinement of KRIs ensure they remain relevant amid changing market conditions.

Finally, it's worth noting the motivational aspect of diligently monitoring KRIs. For investors and financial professionals, KRIs aren't just tools for risk avoidance; they're enablers of optimized performance. By staying informed and prepared, you empower yourself to make strategic decisions that can significantly enhance your returns while keeping risks within an acceptable range. There's a sense of confidence and assurance derived from knowing that potential risks are identified, measured, and managed effectively.

Key Risk Indicators and Metrics form the backbone of a sound risk management framework. These tools allow you to identify potential hazards before they materialize, affording you the opportunity to take preemptive action. They not only help in safeguarding investments but also in seizing opportunities that arise from a well-understood risk landscape. In the end, mastering KRIs means mastering the art of balancing risk and reward, an essential skill for anyone aiming to succeed in the dynamic world of finance and investments.

www.ingramcontent.com/pod-product-compliance
Lightning Source LLC
Chambersburg PA
CBHW030528210326
41597CB00013B/1065